Austrian Architecture and Design
Beyond Tradition in the 1990s

Austrian Architecture and Design
Beyond Tradition in the 1990s

John Zukowsky
Ian Wardropper

The Art Institute of Chicago
Ernst & Sohn

The exhibition has received the honorary pa-
tronage of His Excellency Mr. Franz Vranitzky,
the Federal Chancellor of the Republic of
Austria, His Excellency Mr. Alois Mock, the
Federal Minister of Foreign Affairs of the Republic of Austria, the Honorable Governor of
the State of Illinois, Mr. Jim Edgar, and the
Honorable Mayor of the City of Chicago, Mr.
Richard M. Daley.

The exhibition and book were made possible
by the support of the Gesellschaft der Freun-
de der bildenden Künste, the Creditanstalt-
Bankverein, the Österreichische Länderbank
Aktiengesellschaft, the KLM Royal Dutch Air-
lines, Kimball International, the Architecture
Society Fellows, and the Seymour H. Persky
Fund for Architecture.

The book is a publication of the Ernest R. Graham Study Center for Architectural Drawings
at The Art Institute of Chicago.

Reproductions: Reprogesellschaft Lutz Wahl
mbH, Berlin
Typesetting and printing: Alphabet KG, Berlin
Binding: Buchbinderei Bruno Helm, Berlin

Supervision and design: Axel Menges
Coordination: Dorothea A. Duwe
Editing: Almut Eckell
Production: Fred Willer

Frontispiece: Hans Hollein, Haas-Haus, Vienna,
1985-90. (Photo: Georg Riha, Vienna)

Contents

Foreword

This year marks the bicentennial of the death of Wolfgang Amadeus Mozart (1756-1791), renowned composer and musician, whom many feel was Austria's greatest gift to the history of music. 1991 will witness numerous musical festivals to honor his memory, and by extension, remind everyone of the contributions that he and fellow Austrians have made, not only to music, but also to western culture. Figures such as composer Johann Strauss (1804-1849), psychologist Sigmund Freud (1856-1939), painters Gustav Klimt (1862-1918) and Egon Schiele (1890-1918), architects Johann Bernhard Fischer von Erlach (1656-1723), Josef Hoffmann (1870-1956), Adolf Loos (1870-1933), and Otto Wagner (1841-1918), all made their mark on the history of civilization. But it is particularly the work of those and other turn-of-the-century architects and designers of the Secession movement and the Wiener Werkstätte that most influenced our built environment since these artists and craftsmen were among the forerunners of modern design. Chicago, a city with a rich and creative architectural heritage, particularly from the decades around 1900, has a natural affinity with Vienna.

Just as they had done almost a century before, a number of Austria's contemporary architects and designers are among the leaders of their profession today. In recognition of this The Art Institute of Chicago is therefore pleased to present, in this publication and exhibition, a selection of those Austrian design innovators in order to introduce their works to an American public. In doing this it is our intention to remind all that the visual culture of Austria goes well beyond images of traditional forms that we all too often associate with that nation.

This project also represents the first time that the departments of Architecture and European Decorative Arts combined their resources and talent in a cooperative spirit to help make this exhibition and book a tangible reality for an American audience. I applaud their efforts and hope that other such joint ventures, both within and outside our museum walls, will enable our audience to have the opportunity to gain first-hand experience of the design achievements and philosophies of other cities and nations, past and present.

James N. Wood, Director, The Art Institute of Chicago

Acknowledgments

The idea for this exhibition and book was born in 1989 from discussions with Clemens Coreth, the Austrian Consul General in Chicago, and his wife Sini. Both of them were tirelessly enthusiastic in their support for this project from the start. Their sustained cooperation and efforts were essential to the success of this endeavor. Clemens Coreth himself introduced us to a number of people who made substantial contributions to this project, both intellectually and financially.

Of those who supported this exhibition, we are particularly indebted to Helmut Haschek, Chairman of the Board of Executive Directors and General Manager of the Österreichische Kontrollbank and Sylvia Eisenburger of the Gesellschaft der Freunde der bildenden Künste. The Gesellschaft or Society of the Friends of the Visual Arts gave generous support to this project. The Creditanstalt-Bankverein also supported our efforts and Nikolaus Dreihann-Holenia of that bank was most helpful in that regard. Reinhard Spies arranged for the Österreichische Länderbank Aktiengesellschaft to support our project as well. Transportation support for the couriers and objects on display was provided by KLM Royal Dutch Airlines. Especially helpful in this were: Eric R. Burgoyne, the Director of Passenger Sales for the Midwest Region; Rick Cornelisse, the Marketing and Sales Development Manager for the Midwest; and Frank Maguire, the former Marketing Services Coordinator for the Midwest, and his replacement, Linda Keller. Additional funding from within The Art Institute of Chicago came from the Seymour H. Persky Fund for Architecture and the Architecture Society Fellows: Darcy Bonner, Laurence Booth, Lonn Frye, Michael Glass, Joseph Gonzalez, Bruce Gregga, Marilyn and Wilbert Hasbrouck, Scott Himmel, Helmut Jahn, Seymour Persky, Gordon Lee Pollock, John Schlossman, Kenneth Schroeder, Patrick Shaw, Stanley Tigerman, Robert Weinberg, and Martin Zimmerman. Kimball International made it possible to transport the Bösendorfer piano to Chicago. We gratefully acknowledge the assistance of Mr. Douglas Habig, President of Kimball International, Mr. Anthony P. Habig, Executive Vice-President, and Vic Geiger, also of Kimball, as well as Mr. P. Lemell, Director, Bösendorfer, Vienna, Dr. Radler, Managing Director, Bösendorfer, Vienna, and Mr. James Turner, Bösendorfer SE and Institution Sales Manager.

A successful loan exhibition requires the cooperation of lenders, and the architects and designers who lent items to this exhibit deserve our gratitude. The staff of those various firms were often instrumental in securing specific information and clearance for their pieces as well as allowing access to photographs and documentation, and they deserve special thanks: Gudrun Pleyer and Norbert Müller in Günther Domenig's office; Angela Althaler and Claudia J. Price with Coop Himmelblau; August Sarnitz in the office of Gustav Peichl; Madeleine Jenewein in Hans Hollein's office; Dirk Schmauser of Porsche Design; as well as officers at manufacturing firms which supplied us with products designed by Porsche: Mr. Schoenborn, Grundig AG; Mr. Zettler, Elektrotechn. Fabrik GmbH; Mr. Kleinhappel, Eudora Werke; Mr. Giroletti, PAF. Mr. Lucchesi-Palli of the Alpenländische Veredelungs-Industrie Ges.m.b.H. and Jeanette Bronée of Vitra, New York, all gave valuable advice and generous assistance in transporting objects from their respective firms.

Other people in Vienna, and elsewhere, assisted and advised us on this project, and their help was much appreciated: Peter Noever, Director of the Österreichisches Museum für angewandte Kunst and two of his curators, Christian Witt-Dörring and Verena Formanek; Carl Auböck; Inge Asenbaum; Peter Teichgraber of Prodomo; Matthäus Jiszda; Victor Margolin, Professor of Design at the University of Illinois-Chicago; and Axel Menges, the architecture editor for Ernst & Sohn, as well as Dorothea A. Duwe, Almut Eckell and Fred Willer of the same firm.

In Chicago at our museum, a number of people were supportive of this exhibit and catalog. James N. Wood, our director, gave us his whole-hearted endorsement. The Committee on Architecture was equally enthusiastic: David C. Hilliard (Chairman), James N. Alexander, J. Paul Beitler, Thomas Boodell, Jr., Edwin J. DeCosta, Stanley Freehling, Graham C. Grady, Bruce J. Graham, Neil Harris, Lynn Maddox, Carter H. Manny, Jr., Peter Palumbo, Seymour H. Persky, Mrs. J. A. Pritzker, Harold Schiff, Patrick Shaw, Thomas Theobald, and Stanley Tigerman. The Committee on European Decorative Arts and Sculpture and Classical Art also gave its approbation to our efforts: Mrs. Harold T. Martin (Chairman), Mrs. John Q. Adams, Jr., Mrs. Walter Alsdorf, Mrs. P. Kelley Armour, Mrs. T. Stanton Armour, Bowen Blair, John H. Bryan, Mrs. Henry M. Buchbinder, Mrs. Eugene A. Davidson (honorary), Edwin J. DeCosta, David P. Earle III, Mrs. Paul A. Florian III, Mrs. Michael Galvin, Mrs. Robert Hixon Glore, Mrs. Richard Gottlieb, Mrs. William O. Hunt, Mrs. Fred K. Krehbiel, Kenneth Maier, Mrs. Brooks McCormick, Mrs. Eric Oldberg, Andrew Rosenfield, Mrs. A. Loring Rowe, Mrs. Margaret H. Ryerson, Mrs. Theodore D. Tieken, Mrs. Edgar J. Uihlein, and Mrs. George B. Young.

Finally, staff members of The Art Institute assisted in making this a reality and we are thankful for their hard work in this: Dorothy Schroeder, Assistant Director for Exhibitions and Budget; Susan Rossen, Executive Director of Publications; Robert V. Sharp, Associate Director of Publications; Joseph Cochand in graphics; Mary Solt, Registrar; Mary Mulhern, Associate Registrar; Reynold Bailey, Art Installation; Linda Adelman, Secretary, and Luigi Mumford, Technical Assistant, both in the Department of Architecture; and Marilyn Conrad, Assistant to the Curator, and Bill Gross, Tony Sigel, and Karen Johnson, Technicians, and Kirsten Darnton, Secretary, in the Department of European Decorative Arts and Sculpture and Classical Art. Finally, special thanks to Alice Sabe, the President of the Architecture Society, and the society's board members who worked diligently to organize the opening reception for the exhibition, and to Amy Gold, who was a research assistant for this project as well as the author of the architects' and designers' biographies, the compiler of the bibliography, and writer of the illustration credits.

John Zukowsky, Curator of Architecture

Ian Wardropper, Eloise W. Martin Curator of European Decorative Arts and Sculpture and Classical Art

John Zukowsky
Contemporary Architecture in Austria – At Last, Another Revolution in the Empire

Austria and Vienna, its cultural and political capital, have long been associated with musical and visual accomplishments. But when we think of their built environment, we naturally focus on the fabric of Vienna at the turn of the century, and the work of the early moderns such as Otto Wagner (1841-1918), Josef Hoffmann (1870-1956), Adolf Loos (1870-1933), and others. To many this was the high point of Austrian design during the peak of the Empire before World War I which embraced the current territories of Hungary, Czechoslovakia, and beyond to portions of Poland and the Soviet Union. Architectural professionals and lay enthusiasts alike generally agree that those design efforts were a revolution in the Empire even though those works could also, at times, be interpreted as an extension of Viennese or Austrian national design tendencies. But the output of several Austrian architects practicing today is as revolutionary, if not more so. Yet, these contemporary architects do not receive the recognition given to their ancestors. In many ways, the difficult task of grappling with their design heritage and still going well beyond it and our notions of modernism deserves even greater adulation than that given to the early modernists of Vienna. This essay will, therefore, introduce the recent work of five contemporary Austrian architects in relation to the broader context of design traditions

in that city and others in that nation. It will offer observations on the cultural and intellectual climate, past and present, that catalyzed and continues to drive their distinctive, individualistic approaches to solving architectural problems. But, before we enter their world, it will be helpful for us to briefly review the history of architecture in that country over the past century and, in the process, provide observations about Austria's buildings in relation to her own social and political history.

Austrian Architecture of the 1900s:
The Empire Continues to Strike Back

When one either wanders through the streets of Vienna or visits churches in rural Austria, one is struck by a consistency of attitude toward complexity in pattern and ornament. As Frank Lothar Kroll recently observed in "Ornamental Theory and Practice in the Jugendstil" (*Rassegna,* March 1990), ornament achieved a significant and comparable formal role in both the architecture of the Rococo and Jugendstil. Figures such as Otto Wagner condemned as lifeless repetition the academic sculptures of classical buildings as witnessed in the profusion of caryatids that one can see attached to numerous sites in Vienna. But it is just such an obsession with replication that creates a pattern of appearance, whether in human form or the abstracted shapes favored by the Viennese moderns. It is both the consistently elaborate classicism of mid to late nine-

1. Otto Wagner, Apartment house, Linke Wienzeile 38, Vienna, 1898-99. (Photo: John Zukowsky)
2. Otto Wagner, Apartment house ("Majolika-Haus"), Linke Wienzeile 40, Vienna, 1898-99. (Photo: John Zukowsky)

teenth century buildings there, particularly on the Ringstrasse, as well as the consistently elaborate, if abstracted, surface ornamentalism of the blocky masses of Secession or Jugendstil buildings that characterize Vienna at the peak of the Austro-Hungarian Empire. One can speculate further why elaborate or even busy ornamentalism seems to permeate many of their art forms, even to the point of Gustav Klimt's paintings which can sometimes consist of both patterned and abstractly sculptured surfaces.

In his perceptive article for the *Austrian New Wave* catalog (1980) published by the Institute for Architecture and Urban Studies, long-time Austrian architectural writer Friedrich Achleitner commented on tendencies in Viennese architecture, past and present. He observed that Viennese architects have a predilection for the witty, theatrical, and the idea (rather than reality) of architecture, with Austria almost never a country to foster architectural innovation. His cogent essay analyzes the development of Vienna's architecture up through the 1970s. Yet, it provides no greater recognition of those complexities in design and society, nor does it recognize any Austrian innovativeness which, as we shall see, certainly does exist.

Werner Hoffmann's recent article on "The Style Debate in the Vienna School" (*Rassegna,* March 1990) discusses turn-of-the-century Viennese abstraction and surface pattern in relation to both an interest in like patterns in Byzantine art and the dream theories of Sigmund Freud's *Interpretation of Dreams* pub-

lished in 1900. Hoffmann's citation of dematerialized humanism of Byzantine art is also interesting in that this region has always served as a bridge to the East, and its culture could well be receptive to the idea of abstract patterns popular in Islamic society, even though the Turks themselves were halted here in the siege of Vienna in 1683-85. But this tendency toward design complexity through pattern could also reflect comparable tendencies toward being "Byzantine" in the sense of petty intrigues in Viennese and even Austrian society at the time of the Empire's peak under Franz Joseph I. Even through today the tendency toward overcomplication is carried on from complex varieties of coffee available and other intricacies of café etiquette, through more tangible expressions such as the Baroque-like sculptural masses in recent works of the husband and wife team of Michael Szyszkowitz and Karla Kowalski, to the bizarre busyness of artist Friedensreich Hundertwasser's decorative facades.

Be that as it may, the Empire received its major socio-political shock with the outbreak of the First World War after the assassination of imperial heir Archduke Franz Ferdinand on 28 June 1914. Intertwined with Germany and Turkey, they faced the Allies. All eventually lost the war and much of their domains after the armistice of 11 November 1918, and subsequent treaties of Versailles with Germany on 28 June 1919 and Saint-Germain-en-Laye with Austria on 10 September 1919. The loss of the war signaled the end of the Austro-Hungarian Empire and the

3. Caryatids on the Linke Wienzeile, Vienna. (Photo: John Zukowsky)
4. Otto Wagner, Stadtbahnhof Hietzing, city-railroad station for the imperial court near Schloß Schönbrunn, Vienna, 1894-98. (Photo: John Zukowsky)

pp. 10, 11
5. Friedensreich Hundertwasser, Apartment house, Löwengasse and Kegelgasse, Vienna, 1983-85. (Photo: John Zukowsky)
6. Michael Szyszkowitz and Karla Kowalski, Biotechnological Institute, Technical University, Graz, 1983-90. (Photo: John Zukowsky)

formation of the First Republic of Austria. This attempt at the creation of a democratic government became a struggle between various political entities: Social Democrats, Catholic Christian Socialists, and German nationalist parties. Eventually the Great Depression of the early 1930s led to factional strife and a shift, in 1933, toward an increasingly right-wing and authoritarian, yet fervently nationalistic, government under Chancellor Engelbert Dollfuss. After his assassination in 1934 by pro-Nazis, he was succeeded by Kurt Schuschnigg who went down in history as the Chancellor to reluctantly announce a plebiscite for 13 March 1938, only to have Hitler's troops invade the day before.

As with Weimar Germany in the 1920s and early 30s, fledgling democracy in Austria was meant, in theory, to establish a new socio-political condition with appropriately modern expressions for its built environment. Architects such as Loos and Hoffmann continued to design buildings, many of which were devoid of any ornament; Clemens Holzmeister (1886-1983) built religious and quasi-public buildings in styles ranging from expressionist Gothic through severely modern; and other architects such as Lois Welzenbacher (1889-1955) made their mark with modernist villas throughout the country. But, aside from some of the buildings done for Vienna's Werkbundsiedlung of 1932 and a few scattered commercial and residential buildings there and in other cities, most of the executed projects seem tame when compared with buildings by Germany's

more radical modernists such as Ludwig Mies van der Rohe (1886-1969), Erich Mendelsohn (1887-1953), and Bruno Taut (1880-1938). Even the most visible expression of so-called "Red Vienna" of the twenties – social housing for workers – used decorated massing and details more closely linked in expression to those of the Viennese Secession movement at the turn of the century than to new, stark modernist forms for housing projects in Germany. Moreover, Austrian expatriate architects practicing in America, namely Richard Neutra (1892-1970) and Rudolph Schindler (1887-1953), generally built more radically modernist buildings than their counterparts in Austrian cities. This becomes even more apparent when one recalls their machined interiors of glass and chromesteel furnishings when compared with the mostly wood fixtures and paneling along with the upholstered wood furniture in many Austrian interiors, even those designed by their leading architects.

It seems then that Austria's architects between the world wars were more restrained and somewhat conservative when compared with their German cousins. Perhaps this is because they were searching for a building expression appropriate to their nation's quest for a national identity as suggested by Achleitner in *Austrian New Wave.* He cited Austrian architecture's compromise between classicism and modernism which grew into attempts at a traditional Heimatarchitektur under the nationalist government of Dollfuss. Or, perhaps it is simply because architects too had dif-

7. Adolf Loos with Heinrich Kulka, House on Woinovichgasse, Werkbundsiedlung Vienna, 1930-32. (Photo: John Zukowsky)
8. Paul Geppert and the Wagner Brothers, Building of the Wiener Städtische, Max-Ott-Platz 3, Salzburg, 1932-33, later altered. (Photo: John Zukowsky)

9. Karl Ehn, Karl-Marx-Hof, Heiligenstädter Strasse, Vienna, 1926-30. (Photo: John Zukowsky)
10. Otto Haesler, Siedlung Rothenberg, Kassel, Germany, 1930. (Photo: John Zukowsky)
11. Richard Neutra, Galka Scheyer house, 1880 Blue Heights Road, Los Angeles, California, 1933. Perspective study. (Restricted gift of the Auxiliary Board to The Art Institute of Chicago, 1987.45)
12. Josef Hoffmann, Unidentified office and showroom, c. 1935. Elevations. (Gift of Pamela M. Hoffmann Benson and Mrs. Wolfgang Hoffmann to The Art Institute of Chicago, 1985.139)

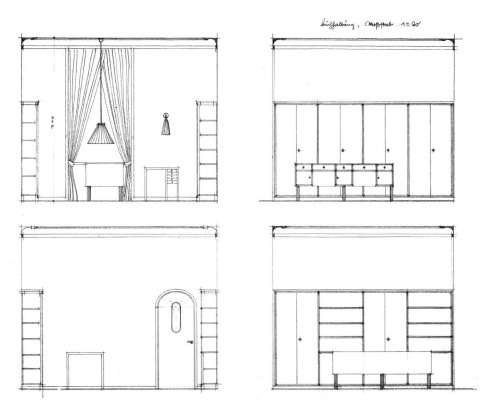

ficulty in dealing with the loss of their Empire and Vienna's pre-eminent position in design and wished to harken back to its glories. The holocaust to follow pushed that design problem into the background as survival moved to the forefront.

During the Second World War, with Austria annexed within the Third Reich after the Anschluss of 1938, architects there suffered the same fate as in Germany and many of the occupied countries. Those who did not flee, or who were not killed in the war, worked to satisfy the Reich's architectural and industrial design needs. One such was the modernist architect Welzenbacher who designed aircraft installations during the war. Of the modernist military industrial complexes that were constructed in this time period, Linz is home to one of the largest and most famous – the former Hermann Göring Steel Works on the Danube from 1938 to 1943, and now the United Austrian Iron and Steel Works (VOEST-Alpine AG) with later additions. One of the most infamous architectural sites of the war is the partly preserved concentration camp near Mauthausen. Established in 1938, it housed more than 200,000 prisoners until it was liberated in May 1945. More than half of them died or were killed here. Equally ominous are the Viennese anti-aircraft defenses built in 1942. These concrete bunkers, often still scarred from bombing raids, serve as powerful reminders within the city's urban fabric of those cataclysmic years.

The closing days of World War II brought the Russian and American ar-

mies into Austria. Along with their British and French counterparts, the four allies occupied the country as they had Germany. In some ways, artificial partitioning of the country helped to lay the groundwork for the postwar development of the nation's distinct regional states: Burgenland, Kärnten, Niederösterreich, Oberösterreich, Salzburg, Steiermark, Tirol, Vienna, and Vorarlberg. And films such as the classic *The Third Man* (1949) remind us that, like Berlin, Vienna herself was divided into Soviet, American, British, and French sectors until the establishment of the Second Republic in 1955.

The architecture of that era dealt with the obvious need for reconstruction of damaged historic monuments, such as Stephansdom, Schloss Schönbrunn, and Palais Schwarzenberg in Vienna, as well as the repair and new construction of housing and commercial facilities. The immediate post-war buildings often looked like their prewar predecessors, and housing projects of the early 1950s by Josef Hoffmann and Sepp Stein, among others, bear a resemblance to either conservative modernist buildings of the twenties or more simplified classical buildings of the thirties. A similar hybrid can be seen in the Chemical Institute building of the Technical University at Graz from the same time period by Karl Raimund Lorenz. It bears the masonry modernism of Lorenz's teacher Hans Poelzig and, at the same time, Aalto-like details in the entrance canopy as well as in the central stairhall.

13. Friedrich Tamms, Anti-aircraft tower in the Auergarten, Vienna, 1942. (Photo: John Zukowsky)
14. Sepp Stein and Carl Machtlinger, Housing on Lainzerstrasse and Kraus Promenade, Vienna, 1951-53. (Photo: John Zukowsky)
15. Josef Hoffmann with Josef Kalbac, Housing on Silbergasse 2-4 and Nusswaldgasse 2, Vienna, 1951. Elevations and site plan. (Gift of Pamela M. Hoffmann Benson to The Art Institute of Chicago, 1985.122)

GST. 1, GST. 2, GST. 3/1, GST. 3/2, GEM. WIEN, KATASTRALGEM. UNTERDÖBLING

MASSTAB 1:100

ANSICHT SILBERGASSE

BAUWERBER: PLANVERFASSER: BAUFÜHRER:

WIEN IM FEBRUAR 1951

The departure of the allied forces from a now neutral Austria, established by the Staatsvertrag of 1955, permitted further development of its location as a bridge between the East and West especially as the Cold War intensified in the 1960s and 70s. And this socio-political or socio-cultural neutrality enabled the country to prosper, and its architects to find an expression suited to their national and individual tastes, all doubtless catalyzed by the flowering of a liberal democracy under Chancellor Bruno Kreisky. It was in this era that Johann Staber built the Vienna International Center in a modernist vein similar to the works of Aalto and Le Corbusier to accommodate the UNO-City in 1973-1976 for agencies of the United Nations situated here in recognition of the pivotal location of Vienna between East and West. Roland Rainer (born 1910), educated at the Technical University in Vienna, became one of the city's leading modernist architects, whose own interests involved prefabrication, and its Chief Planning Officer from 1958 to 1963. Others such as Wilhelm Holzbauer (born 1930), a student of Holzmeister and one of Austria's leading practitioners of modernism in the classical sense, received numerous prominent private and public commissions including, as with Otto Wagner, a number of subway stations. Yugoslavian Boris Podrecca (born 1941) and Rob Krier (born 1938 in Luxemburg) are among those living in Vienna who became part of an international reaction to monumental, often impersonal, modernist buildings, doing so-called contextual and historically-referenced post-modernist works. Hermann Czech (born 1936) took that historicism to a new level of technical perfection by evoking nineteenth-century Vienna in his interiors and furnishings in his Restaurant Salzamt of 1983 and, most recently, in his remodelings of the Hotel Palais Schwarzenberg in the mid to late 1980s.

Unlike that apparent clinging to the visual traditions of the Empire, some other architects used the architectural heritage of Austria, in general, and Vienna, in particular, as a starting point. Perhaps the cult of the individual promoted after the 1968 student riots well into the 70s, an international phenomenon, had something to do with their appearance now. They drew upon those earlier traditions as well as aspects of international modernism popularized in the postwar period, to create their own very powerfully individualistic design vocabularies.

Good examples are: Günther Domenig's expressionist Z-Bank in Vienna from 1975 to 1979; Hans Hollein's jewel-like Retti candle shop from 1964 to 1965 and the first Schullin jewelry shop from 1972 to 1974, and various branches of the Austrian travel agency from 1976, all in Vienna; and Gustav Peichl's famed broadcasting stations, high-tech but individualistically modern, in Dornbirn, Innsbruck, Linz, Salzburg from 1968 to 1972, and Graz from 1979 to 1981. Their pioneering, in some sense, laid the groundwork for the experiments of other younger architects like Wolf Prix and Helmut Swiczinsky, both of the firm of Coop Himmelblau, and Heinz Tesar.

16. Karl Raimund Lorenz, Chemical Institute, Technical University, Graz, 1952-60. (Photo: John Zukowsky)
17. Johann Staber, Vienna International Center, UNO-City, Wagramer Strasse, Vienna, 1973 to 1976. (Photo courtesy: Bundespressedienst Wien)

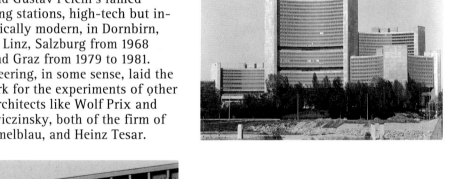

18. Hermann Czech, Hotel Palais Schwarzenberg, Schwarzenbergplatz 9, Vienna, 1984. Bar. (Photo courtesy: Hotel Palais Schwarzenberg)
19. Günther Domenig, Z-Bank, Favoritenstrasse 118, Vienna, 1978-79. (Photo: John Zukowsky)
20. Gustav Peichl, ORF broadcasting studio, Buchgraben 51, Graz, 1978-81. (Photo: John Zukowsky)

Those five architectural firms are, without doubt, the strongest, individualistic architectural design talents in Austria. Although there are many other competent architects, some of whom have already been mentioned, none is as consistently individualistic. Some younger architects even seem to be followers of those five design talents, or too tied to the forms of either traditional modernism or the design traditions of the Empire and turn-of-the-century Austria. Although they may well have a promising future, their current work cannot be compared with the more mature work of those five firms. In many ways, these five firms are the strong designers that Austria's modern movement lacked in the 1920s, and their growth here is tangible indication of the cultural and intellectual liberalization that took place in Vienna and Austria under its postwar democracy, particularly in the 1970s under the socialist government of famed Chancellor Kreisky. The current leadership of Chancellor Franz Vranitzky since 1986 has continued this tradition of support for cultural individualism, providing a sympathetic environment for these five and others to develop their design talents. And their design work is, as we shall see, even more revolutionary than that of their ancestors from the turn of the century. This is especially so since these design visions are not simply paper fantasies. As with their Secessionist ancestors, they also have built expressions of their ideas. Yet they, too, share a consistency of vision and a complexity of expression.

Five for the Future, Out of the Past

Those five design firms are not a cohesive group who exhibit and publish together, such as the New York Five and Chicago Seven of the 1970s and 80s. They are much more independent in design philosophy than that. But they do share a common point in using national design traditions from the early 1900s and the vocabulary and materials of modernism as points of departure to create their own expressions of design for the future. As such, some have been labeled "deconstructivist" when they have been practicing their own forms of disassembled and mannerist modernism long before that term was fashionable. Even the most radical of these five, however, cannot completely turn their backs on traditions of complexity and ornamentalism, either consciously or unconsciously. It may seem contradictory, but tendencies of complexity and continuity are characteristics of the work of those five firms. In some ways, these designers are also voices in the wilderness, often with greater recognition of their design abilities abroad than in their own country. This could partly explain why their works are few in number and often small in scale when compared with their counterparts in, say, France, Germany, Japan, or the USA. Although they have some large commissions, their general output of smaller projects lends a nice comparison with the small-scale, jewel-like projects of their Secessionist predecessors in the early 1900s. With that background in mind, we can now examine the recent work of these firms within the context of their own past experiences as well as their design heritage.

Gustav Peichl

Gustav Peichl's work is, among the five discussed here, the most closely linked to the traditions of the modern movement from before the Second World War. One need only cite his ship-like PEA (phosphate elimination plant) in Berlin-Tegel from 1979 to 1983 with regard to the Le Corbusier-like imagery of modern architecture as a machine for living, the tradition of modern industrial forms in Berlin, and the popular association that we have of streamlined automobiles, airplanes, and ocean liners of the early thirties with modernism. But Peichl's link with the modern movement in the classical sense is no great surprise. He was a student of Clemens Holzmeister from 1949 to 1953, and Holzmeister's

work after the war (such as the 1964 Holy Family parish church in Vienna) was done in the spirit of prewar modern buildings. As with Ludwig Mies van der Rohe and other modernists, Peichl prides himself on making artistic yet good buildings – Baukunst.

Although Peichl has been designing buildings since the early 1960s, with notable early jobs ranging from the interior design of Caravelle airplanes for Austrian Airlines in 1962 through the Austrian pavilion at the 1964 New York World's Fair, his most famous commissions began in 1968 when he designed broadcasting studios and other facilities for the ORF (Austrian Radio). These stations, sometimes affectionately termed "Peichl-Kuchen" or "Peichl-Cakes", are masterpieces of high-tech detailing and expressionist planning equal to anything done by Erich Mendelsohn. Their complex appearance projects the imagery of complicated technology. But Peichl, a well-known caricaturist, also shows his sense of humor in his witty

21. Gustav Peichl, Phosphate elimination plant, Buddestrasse, Berlin-Tegel, 1979-83. (Photo: Uwe Rau)
22. Gustav Peichl, ORF broadcasting studio, Innsbruck, 1972. Axonometric view.

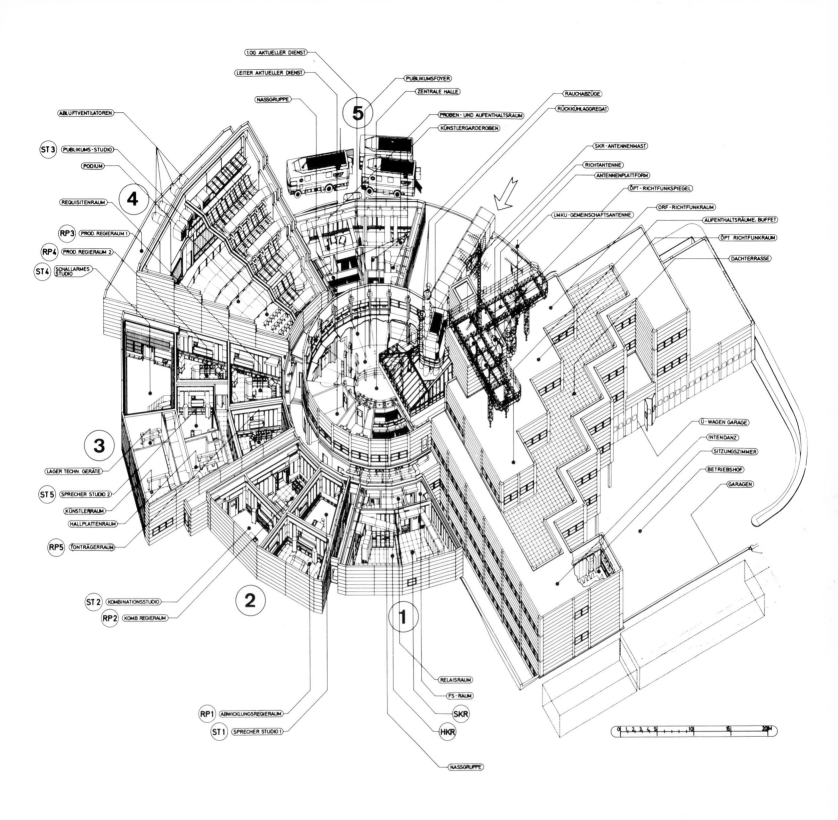

ABLUFTVENTILATOREN

ST 3 PUBLIKUMS-STUDIO
PODIUM

REQUISITENRAUM

RP 3 PROD. REGIERAUM 1
RP 4 PROD. REGIERAUM 2
ST 4 SCHALLARMES STUDIO

3

LAGER TECHN. GERÄTE

ST 5 SPRECHER STUDIO 2
KÜNSTLERRAUM
HALLPLATTENRAUM

RP 5 TONTRÄGERRAUM

ST 2 KOMBINATIONSSTUDIO
RP 2 KOMB. REGIERAUM

2

RP 1 ABWICKLUNGSREGIERAUM
ST 1 SPRECHER STUDIO 1

NASSGRUPPE

1.OG AKTUELLER DIENST
LEITER AKTUELLER DIENST

5

PUBLIKUMSFOYER
ZENTRALE HALLE

PROBEN- UND AUFENTHALTSRAUM
KÜNSTLERGARDEROBEN

4

RAUCHABZÜGE
RÜCKKÜHLAGGREGAT

SKR-ANTENNENMAST
RICHTANTENNE
ANTENNENPLATTFORM
ÖPT-RICHTFUNKSPIEGEL
ORF-RICHTFUNKRAUM
LMKU-GEMEINSCHAFTSANTENNE
AUFENTHALTSRÄUME, BUFFET
ÖPT. RICHTFUNKRAUM
DACHTERRASSE

Ü-WAGEN GARAGE
INTENDANZ
SITZUNGSZIMMER
BETRIEBSHOF
GARAGEN

1

RELAISRAUM
FS-RAUM
SKR
HKR

NASSGRUPPE

0 1 2 3 4 5   10   15   20M

19

design of some of the ventilator shafts for these buildings as medieval metallic tents. The success of these broadcasting facilities led to other commissions for ORF, from the dramatic, yet minimalist, sunken radio satellite station in Aflenz from 1976 to 1979 to the 1982-83 archives building for the ORF in Vienna. The archives building is an addition to a comparably designed and masonry constructed building of 1935-39 by Clemens Holzmeister, Heinrich Schmid, and Hermann Aichinger. The materials and massing of Peichl's addition coexist well with the original, designed by his teacher. Moreover, the simple, block-like mass of the stuccoed exterior and the use of the grid in a decorative pattern within the interior acknowledge traditions of the Viennese Secession and particularize this building to its Vienna site. Even more than that, the massing and details prefigure similarities in his most recent works.

His competition entry of 1990 for the Kammerspiele in Munich as well as his newly executed museums and exhibit spaces in Bonn and Frankfurt display simplified massing akin to that of the early moderns from Vienna, 1900. The earlier medieval tents of ORF studios at Salzburg and Graz have become, at the Kunsthalle in Bonn, pop-tents in a pop-landscape, while functioning also as skylight towers in the sculpture garden atop the building. The extension to the Städel museum in Frankfurt, with its central rotunda in the tradition of many institutional buildings such as this, provides a simple and dignified exhibition pavilion as does the Secession building in Vienna by Joseph Maria Olbrich from 1897. Peichl's links with tradition are even stronger in the 1989 remodeling of the Kunstforum of the Länderbank in Vienna, its design details consciously similar to those of Hoffmann and Olbrich.

23. Gustav Peichl, Archives building of the ORF, Argentinierstrasse 30 a, Vienna, 1982-83. (Photo: Ali Schafler)
24. Gustav Peichl, Radio satellite station, Aflenz, Austria, 1976-79.

25. Gustav Peichl, Kunstforum of the Länder-bank, Vienna, 1989.
26. Gustav Peichl, Kammerspiele, Munich, 1990. Model of the competitive entry. (Photo: Schwingenschlögl)
27. Gustav Peichl, Kunsthalle, Bonn, begun 1986. Model.

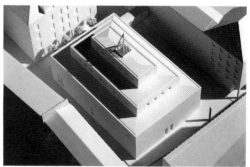

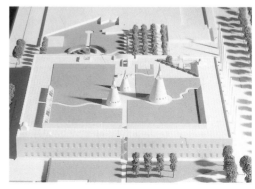

28. Gustav Peichl, Rehearsal stage for the Burgtheater, Vienna, project, 1990. Section.

Even though Peichl started his career as a modernist, we have seen in his more recent work a shift to accommodate contextual features related to the traditions of historic buildings as well as, in particular, his Viennese heritage. His very latest projects, however, seem to bring him a bit closer to his own roots of individual expression that adeptly combines Viennese tradition and the principles of the modern movement. His proposed rehearsal space for the Burgtheater in Vienna bears the same skylight abstracted tent of the Kammerspiele over the theater's central stairhall with the two performance spaces situated off this core. The segmented arch roofs of those two spaces remind one of similarly roofed industrialized buildings from the 1920s. Even more modernist is his recently proposed EVN communications center near Vienna in Maria-Enzersdorf. This Corbusier-like structure is an addition to a slab building that Peichl himself designed and built in 1960. The combination of a slab with this tapering, horizontal mass is reminiscent of Corbusier's concepts for the United Nations building in New York from 1947 to 1953 which was executed by Harrison and Abramowitz. In Peichl's case, the building's curvilinear shape in three dimensions is a response to the function of the auditorium space housed within.

Over the past three decades Peichl's work has matured into a comfortable ac-ceptance of both Vienna's architectural traditions and his own individualistic, yet modernist, heritage. The latest works and, in particular, the EVN communications center, draw upon the best of both worlds to create very simple yet strong solutions to design problems.

Günther Domenig

Günther Domenig has long been considered to be the leader of a so-called "Graz School" of design philosophy. This supposed school of thought was often said to be a strong, independent regional architectural statement as opposed to the more traditional architecture of Vienna during the 1960s and 70s. Books such as the *Grazer "Schule" Architektur-Investitionen* (1986), and *Architektur aus Graz,* which accompanied the 1987-89 Europalia exhibit, and interesting articles by Peter Cook, "Vienna : Graz" and Peter Blundell Jones, "Graz", both in a special issue about Austrian architecture in *The Architectural Review* (December 1988), examined this situation which some might say is comparable to other intercity rivalries in culture and architecture, such as New York and Chicago, Moscow and Leningrad, or Glasgow and London. That Graz, for whatever many social, geographic, and cultural reasons, is very different from Vienna is obvious. More specifically, Blundell Jones' article points out an important difference in architec-

PROBEBUEHNE
BURGTHEATER

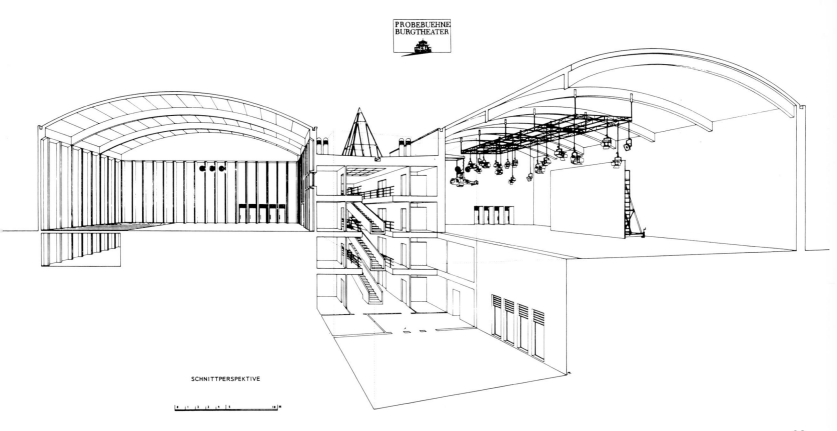

SCHNITTPERSPEKTIVE

29,30. Günther Domenig, Z-Bank, Favoriten-strasse 118, Vienna, 1975-79. Interiors. (Photos: John Zukowsky)
31. Günther Domenig, Multipurpose hall, Georgigasse 84, Graz, 1974-77.
32. Günther Domenig, Rikki Reiner boutique, Alter Platz 1, Klagenfurt, 1983.

tural education between Vienna and Graz in postwar years. He says that Vienna's educational system is dominated by the master class, the single "superstar" teacher whose "party line" is taught to the followers, whereas a comparable situation did not exist in Graz. He states: "The very lack of party lines and master classes has been essential to the nature of architecture in Graz: the atmosphere is free, optimistic, progressive. They do not stumble under the cultural burden of Vienna: the feeling that one can only add footnotes to the work of Wagner and Loos, often with an ironic wink."

Although this may well be true, it is to Günther Domenig that all the younger "individualists" in Austria must owe a great deal of gratitude for paving the way with his own expression of modernism. It is interesting that his buildings have an individual look, yet hybridized nature, akin to some anthropomorphic, metabolist Japanese and American ar-

chitects such as Kisho Kurokawa and Bart Prince. Perhaps this eclectic individualism was a quality encouraged by Domenig's teachers from 1953 to 1959 at the Technical University in Graz such as Karl Raimund Lorenz, whose own buildings, we have noted, are hybridized moderns. One may even say that, as with Peichl, Domenig's Graz buildings done in partnership with Eilfried Huth, such as the Catholic College of Education from the mid 1960s, and his own multipurpose hall of the mid 1970s, along with the already mentioned Z-Bank in Vienna of the mid to late 1970s, all bear an individualized approach to modernism that is also heavily expressive. The Z-Bank itself bears a sculpture of the architect's own hand, enlarged to superhuman size, at work visually molding the building's interior "pasta of pipes". In relation to eclectic or hybridized tendencies, Domenig's more recent work can be expressionist as well as classi-

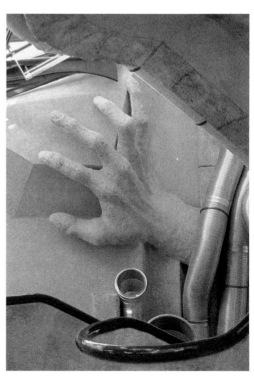

cally modernist, and also, as termed today, deconstructivist.

Buildings such as his newly completed additions to the Technical University are straightforwardly modernist as is the 1988 power station at Unzmarkt. The 1983 boutique for Rikki Reiner in Klagenfurt is more expressionistic, vaguely reminiscent of dynamic interior spaces from the famed set design for the *Cabinet of Dr. Caligari* in 1920. Even more dynamic is the exterior remodeling and internal manipulation of planes and structural members in his eye-catching 1987 addition to the Funder building in St. Veit.

The St. Veit building consists of a steel, metal screen, glass and plexiglas facade that encases the street facade of an existing building. This is the head office of the Funder company which specializes in paper and wood related products, including laminated and pressed board. The spaces created serve as product in-

formation display areas, seminar rooms for employees, and an entertaining area in the main lobby, complete with bar, moving serving ledge, kitchen and toilets. The construction relies, appropriately enough, on industrial materials but the feeling one gets is that of dynamic dematerialization comparable to that of expressionist spaces. The exterior texture of the slightly rusted steel, varnished and sealed after being exposed to weather for several weeks, is especially striking.

If Domenig invoked the dynamism of industrial imagery through active manipulation of materials in his Funder building, he uses concrete and steel in his own Steinhaus or Stone-House, begun 1983-86 on a lake in Steindorf in southern Austria, to evoke memories of the region's craggy landscape. Therefore, the angular poured concrete structure of the house will hold angular steel pods for living, designed in emulation of the

comparably shaped rocky landscape that he sketched in 1981. Of particular interest is his Nix-Nux-Nix light sculpture. This was first designed for a branch of the Z-Bank in Graz, 1981-83, but the architect liked it so much, he decided to expand and develop the design of this fantasy metal bird for his own home. This fantastic expressionistic sculpture appears as if it is some futuristic bird of prey or maquette for an alien spacecraft in some science fiction film. Another especially beautiful, but simpler, expressive form is the 1982 curvilinear wood structure bridge and dock, as well as a slide into the adjacent lake.

In all, then, Domenig's work remains as fresh and as powerful as it was some thirty years ago. His highly individualistic modernism paved the way for similar freedom of architectural expression by younger architects today. Yet his fre-

quently complex spaces and forms of architectural expression relate, at least superficially and perhaps unconsciously, to the historic traditions of complexity in design in Austria.

Hans Hollein

Hans Hollein is the best known of contemporary Austrian architects in the United States. This is possibly because he has already constructed spaces there in the Richard Feigen Gallery in New York from 1967 to 1969, the 1974-76 installation design in the Cooper-Hewitt Museum, of the inaugural show, "Man transFORMS", and the Ludwig Beck store in Trump Tower from 1981 to 1983 which, unfortunately, has been dismantled. It could also be because he has created a number of striking design items – glass-

33. Günther Domenig, Power station on the Mur River, Unzmarkt, Austria, 1988.

34. Hans Hollein, Second store for the Schullin Jewelers, Kohlmarkt 7, Vienna, 1981-82. (Photo: John Zukowsky)

ware, silverware, furniture, and ceramics that are marketed internationally, all designed in the spirit of his statement that "Everything is architecture". But, his connection to the United States goes back to student days. After studying with Clemens Holzmeister in Vienna, he came to Chicago from 1958 to 1959 to study at the Illinois Institute of Technology. The next year, 1959-60, he spent in graduate study at the University of California, Berkeley. It was after those advanced studies that he began a series of striking photomontages of conceptual projects, much in the technical spirit of presentations by Ludwig Mies van der Rohe and his colleagues and students at IIT. Except Hollein's photomontages of the early and mid 1960s were usually fantasy, pop-culture projects such as placing an aircraft carrier-city in a rolling rural landscape or a Rolls Royce grill

within the skyline of Manhattan. Those clever photomontages were acquired by private collectors and museums alike, and they may well have catalyzed his early visibility in art and architecture circles in America. Additional recognition in the States could also have come from his teaching experiences at Washington University in St. Louis from 1963 to 1964 and in 1966.

In Vienna he also taught at the Hochschule für angewandte Kunst and built a number of projects that, in scale and attention to detail, bear positive comparison with the jewel-box banks that Louis Sullivan did in the first decades of the twentieth century. Hollein's projects such as the Schullin jewelry stores, the second of which utilizes his visual trademark of the large archaic rounded pediment supported by slender columns, often have design details of elegant pro-

35. Hans Hollein, Primary school, Köhlergasse 9, Vienna, 1979-89.
36. Hans Hollein, Apartment house, Rauchstrasse 8, Berlin-Tiergarten, 1983. (Photo: John Zukowsky)

37. Hans Hollein, Kulturforum, Berlin, project, 1983. Perspective view. (Gift of Hans Hollein through Mr. and Mrs. Jay A. Pritzker to The Art Institute of Chicago, 1989.229)

portions and lavish materials. Attenuated forms also appear as seen in the palm trees of his Austrian travel agencies. A variety of lush materials, and attention to jewel-like detail comparable to that of Loos, Wagner or Hoffmann, all characterize the works of these inner-city Viennese projects.

But Hollein's architectural oeuvre includes larger jobs that range from a primary school in Köhlergasse in Vienna designed in 1979 through housing in Berlin from 1983 in conjunction with the Internationale Bauausstellung. Larger scale urban commissions were built or projected, ranging from his well-known Museum Abteiberg in Mönchengladbach, Germany, from 1972 to 1982 through his 1983 proposal for a cultural forum between Berlin's Neue National-galerie by Ludwig Mies van der Rohe and Staatsbibliothek by Hans Scharoun. In all of those projects an emphasis is made on the creation of a multiplicity of spatial and textural experiences. These range from the school being designed as a mini-village, to the variety of planes and materials used in the Berlin apartment house, to the Mönchengladbach museum being planned as a new town center with separate buildings, through the cultural center in Berlin being designed as a connecting communal space between major urban monuments designed by Mies and Scharoun. Hollein's interest in this multifaceted spatial and structural experience continues and even intensifies in very recent projects.

His newly completed Museum für Moderne Kunst in Frankfurt, a commission

earned in a 1982 competition, fills a difficult, triangular site housed within an urbanistically rigid shell that is highly colored and sculptural in a way similar to the overall feeling of his contemporary Berlin apartment. Even more complex than that, and in keeping with the increasing complexity in his work thus far, is his recently finished Haas-Haus in Vienna.

The Haas-Haus is a multi-use commercial building for offices, shops mostly organized around a central atrium, and restaurant services atop and in the prominent reflective glass turret opposite the famed Stephansdom. This commercial complex is Hollein's largest project in Vienna built, incidentally, within the confines of the original Roman encampment near the corner of the Roman wall. Hollein's curved turret of glass reminds one of its urban archaeological heritage as well as redefines a prominent urban corner which was removed when the square was widened after buildings were damaged in World War II. There is a profusion of richly refined materials within and outside the building, from reflective glass, various marbles, masonry, stainless steel, and painted steel, all beautifully detailed. The building and its less than reserved appearance has received much criticism in Vienna's architectural scene for not being sufficiently visually respectful of the nearby cathedral. Yet the reflection of the adjacent historic buildings in its glass shell heightens one's awareness of the historic importance of this site and provides a visually stimulating urban focal point in

Vienna's old center. The atrium space itself is reminiscent of other large circular and semi-circular spaces back to the famous Guggenheim Museum designed in 1944 by Frank Lloyd Wright. In fact, the Guggenheim is doubtless the starting point for Hollein's spectacular project to build an art museum within the Mönchberg hill of Salzburg.

This project began its life as the premiated entry to a 1989 competition for an art museum in Salzburg and it was modified, in 1990, to be a Guggenheim museum in that site. Hollein's original plan had the visitor enter a cave-like procession of somewhat historicized spaces intended to house antique and medieval art. These have been rearranged to accommodate the Guggenheim's interest in twentieth century art. But, in both cases, the dramatic atrium seemingly carved and blasted out of the mountain will be the focal point, much as the atrium space in the Haas-Haus and the ultimate

inspirational source, Wright's own Guggenheim Museum. The only evidences of any construction happening in this environment will be the skylights atop the Mönchberg and the gilt elevator shaft on the mountain that marks the museum entrance below. The building will have a total area of some 190,000 square feet and is projected to cost about 90 million dollars, with substantial support to be provided by the Austrian government. If all goes well, this fantastic solution to building, as Hollein has said, "a museum in the rock," within the overly historic and stultefyingly historicized Salzburg will be done in 1995.

In Hollein's career thus far we have seen his work over the past three decades move from the traditions of design inspiration and detail of the early Viennese moderns to using the later work of famed individualist moderns such as Frank Lloyd Wright as a point of departure for his own inventive adaptations

38. Hans Hollein, Museum für Moderne Kunst, Frankfurt, 1982-1991. Model. (Photo: Georg Riha)

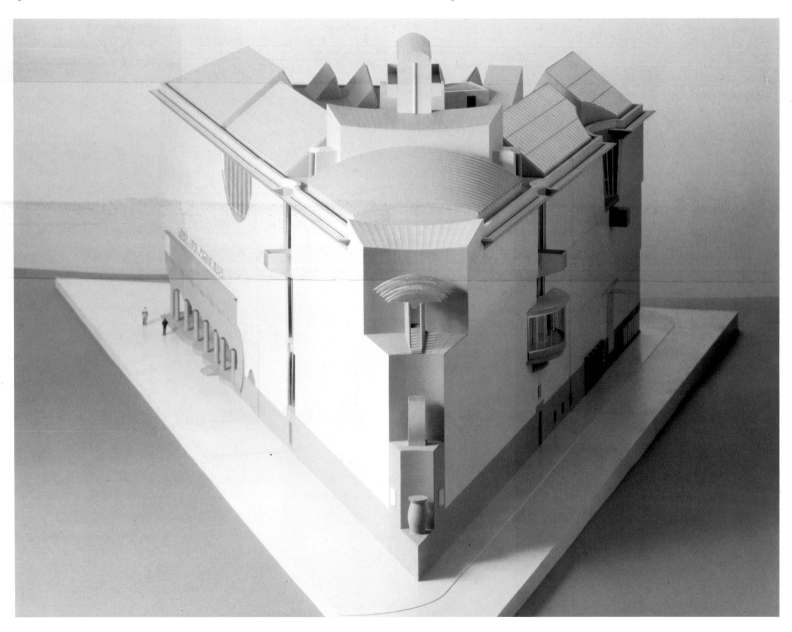

39. Heinz Tesar, Parish church, Kleinarl, Salzburg. 1977-86. (Photo: Margherita Krischanitz)

of form. In both old and new works, his interest lies in perfecting design detail, perhaps as much a legacy from his IIT days as well as Vienna's historic environment. He also provides the visitor with dramatic and complex visual experiences. Those detail and spatial qualities are characteristics that he continually refines in his projects. This complexity of spatial, structural, and material experience is just as intense as in the more overtly designed spatial and structural complexes by Domenig, even though Hollein's vocabulary of design does not seem, on the surface, to be as individually outlandish.

Heinz Tesar

Compared with Peichl, Domenig, and Hollein's developing practices over the past thirty years, Tesar is a relative newcomer. Yet his early training is, in some ways, comparable to theirs. He studied in Vienna with noted modernist architect Roland Rainer from 1961 to 1965. (Rainer built metal and glass buildings there such as the Böhler-Haus of 1956-58 at Elisabethstrasse 12 and the technologically modernist ORF center of 1969-75 on Würzburggasse.) With both his train-

ing within the discipline of modernism and his architectural education heightened by working in Hamburg, Munich and Amsterdam from the late 1950s through the early 1970s, he established independent practice in Vienna in 1973. His projects and ideas were first introduced to an American audience in the traveling exhibit *Austrian New Wave Architecture* (1980). Of the six participants in the exhibit, his is the work that has risen to the forefront of our world today, going beyond the contextual classicists shown there like Rob Krier and Hermann Czech. Some of Tesar's early buildings are the Parish church Unternberg in Lungau/Salzburg from 1976 to 1979, the Mortuary chapel complex in Kleinarl/Salzburg from 1979 to 1986, and the firestation in Perchtoldsdorf in Vienna from 1983 to 1985. These works are characterized by his sensitivity to the design traditions of the landscape or context of the site, but very often we can see references to the powerful, simple spatial massing and the repetitive geometric decoration found in Viennese Secessionist architecture. This almost historicist decorative detailing finds closest expression in the stuccoed facade of his Schömer-Haus in Klosterneuburg near Vienna from 1985 to 1987.

The Schömer-Haus is the office site of one of Austria's building supply equipment companies. The commission was won in competition among Tesar, Rob Krier, and Adolf Krischanitz. Tesar provided the client with a building whose simple, massive facades, similar in design feeling to that of Otto Wagner's Lupus clinic of 1910-13 on Montlearstrasse 37 in Vienna, are highlighted on the first two floors by complex ornamental stucco work. This was done by spooning out the concrete à la "Schlagobers" or the whipped cream of many Austrian desserts. More seriously, sculptured stucco work of this technique parallels that found in the base of the famous Secession building of 1897. The interior, however, is another matter. As with the Hollein projects, this centralized lobby atrium bears comparison with the Guggenheim Museum, especially since the client's contemporary Austrian art collection is on display throughout the building. More important, in terms of design needs, the large stairhall was also meant to serve as a community space and it has been the site of musical and theatrical performances since its construction.

If Tesar's projects, thus far, have concentrated on a mixture of modernist and early Viennese images, two of his latest works also continue as hybrids of historic and modernist associations. The first of these is the rooftop apartment designed for a violinist in Linz after 1985 but finished 1990. This appropriately domed termination of an existing classical building provides the apartment with a grand entrance space. The apartment itself has custom designed furniture including, suitably enough, a beautifully lacquered violin display case to house the owner's "Stradivarins". That piece and some of the remaining custom furniture is based on Tesar's study of an embryonic, amoeba-like form that can be seen in a number of his watercolor sketches. Much as Louis H. Sullivan developed the idea of the "Seed-Germ" which was the basis of all ornament, be it natural or man-made, Tesar uses this embryonic form as the basis of life in his projects within his preliminary concept sketches for the job. His latest work, the successful 1989 competitive entry to design a municipal office building and police station for St. Gall in Switzerland, literalizes the embryo or seed shape in the curvilinear plan for the police station adjacent to the longitudinal rectangular mass of the office building. This massive office complex, though unornamented

40. Heinz Tesar, Mortuary chapel, Kleinarl, Salzburg, 1979-86. Exterior. (Photo Margherita Krischanitz)
41. Heinz Tesar, Mortuary chapel, Kleinarl, Salzburg. Interior showing the "Table of Death" designed to support the coffin. (Photo: Margherita Krischanitz)

in its modernist strip-windowed elevation, sits on a base ornamented with regularized indentations as shown in his competition drawing. One will have to wait until the building is constructed for a final assessment, but it looks as if Tesar is telling us that the modernism of the 1920s and even of today symbolically rests on the pioneering work of the early Viennese moderns.

Tesar's work may seem, at first glance, to be much simpler, more historically oriented, and not as daring as the mature works of Peichl, Domenig, and Hollein. It may seem that the complexities really only come through subtle details, such as the spoon-sculpted decorations of the Schömer facade. It may be deceptively easy, then, to dismiss the work as not being sufficiently bold in expressiveness of structure and spatiality. Yet, his Schömer-Haus provides visitors and workers alike with a surprising vertical spatial experience that contrasts with the horizontal, relatively sober facade that hides it. Considering the fact that he had been in practice only about ten years before this was built, it represents a very positive contribution to the country's architectural environment – one that is certainly more positive than those of a number of other architects his age and younger. The Linz apartment provides both a logical termination for

an historic building as well as a distinctive, yet modern, organizing space for the apartment's plan. The St. Gall project, though severely modern in Tesar's simple line drawings, may well witness an increasingly complex spatial and psychological design development as the final building develops and grows from the sketchy embryo into another grand atrium space.

Coop Himmelblau

The firm of Coop Himmelblau began in 1968 with Wolf D. Prix, Helmut Swiczinsky, and Rainer Michael Holzer (Holzer left the group in 1971). Both Prix and Swiczinsky studied at the Technical University in Vienna. Their early works of the seventies were sculptural or conceptual projects, much like those of colleague firms such as Haus-Rucker-Co. Coop Himmelblau's early work involved their quest to use the power of fantasy to lighten or dematerialize architecture or "to make architecture light and fluctuating like clouds". In an interview within the Viennese architectural journal *Umriss,* 1 & 2 (1989), they comment on their inclusion in the 1988 *Deconstructivist Architecture* exhibit at the Museum of Modern Art in New York by stating, "We stand by the term as well as by this

42. Heinz Tesar, Schömer-Haus, Aufeldstrasse 17-23, Klosterneuburg, Austria, 1985-87. Exterior. (Photo: Zumtobel)
43. Heinz Tesar, Schömer-Haus, Klosterneuburg. Interior of the elliptical hall. (Photo: Zumtobel)

pp. 36, 37
44. Coop Himmelblau, Law office of Schuppich, Sporn und Winischhofer, Falkestrasse 6, Vienna, 1988. Exterior. (Photo: Gerald Zugmann)
45. Coop Himmelblau, Law office of Schuppich Sporn und Winischhofer, Vienna. Conference room. (Photo: Gerald Zugmann)

exhibition." Yet they pursued their own theory of architectural dematerialization in the 1970s and 80s much as James Wines of SITE concurrently developed his own philosophy of de-architecture that decomposes and destructs his buildings. Writers such as Otto Kapfinger in *Architectural Review* (December 1988) and Frank Werner in *A & U* (July 1989) liken their work to other anti-classical tendencies in architectural history, and their work, indeed, seems as if it is fin-de-siècle mannerism or distortion of modernism much as Art Nouveau distorted classicism. Prix himself has recently talked about their initial design process as being motivated by being able "to draw with one's eyes closed", a "psychogram" of the future space being designed (*Newsline,* the newsletter of Columbia University's School of Architecture, September 1990). One is hard-pressed not only to restrain from making observations about the Freudian na-

ture of their design process, but also to cite earlier, yet very similar, precedents of interest in the unconscious dream world by early modern artists and, more precisely, the automatic doodling or automatic drawing, practiced by the Dadaists and Surrealists of the 1920s and 30s.

If psychological automatism and dematerialization are two keys to understanding Coop Himmelblau's design, then a third is art. The firm experimented with conceptual pieces such as the "Hot Flat" of 1978 and the 1980 temporary installation of a forty-foot high sculptural "Wing on Fire" in Graz. These were the first specific projects to angrily dematerialize form, and that aggressive attitude toward design is manifested in the Viennese bar called Roter Engel or Red Angel that they designed in 1981 on Rabensteig 5. Forms in the bar pierced architectural planes within the space. Their buildings and spaces seem to defy our notions of

46. Coop Himmelblau, Funder factory 3, St. Veit an der Glan, Austria, 1988-89. Exterior. (Photo: Gerald Zugmann)
47. Coop Himmelblau, Funder factory 3, St. Veit an der Glan. Interior. (Photo: Gerald Zugmann)

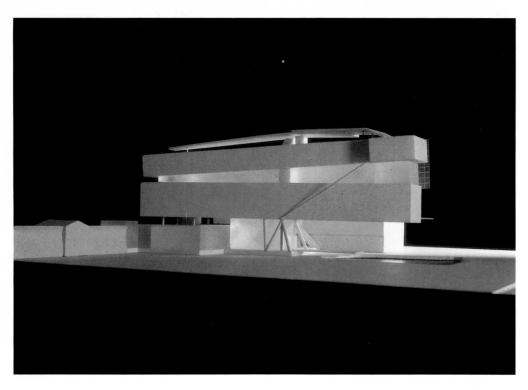

48. Coop Himmelblau, Gartenhotel Altmanns-dorf, Vienna, 1990. Model. (Photo: Gerald Zug-mann)
49. Coop Himmelblau, Gartenhotel Altmanns-dorf, Vienna. Site plan.

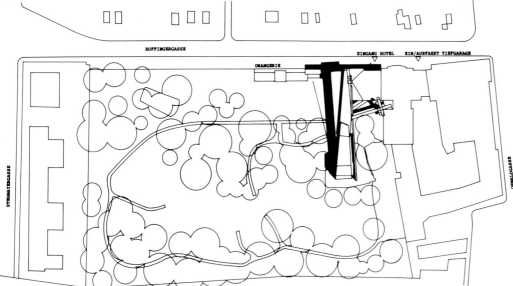

time and space, and the architects them-selves have claimed that "Our architec-ture can be found where thoughts move faster than hands to grasp it." Their buildings capture a moment in a contin-uum of time, much as Futurist artists of the early 1920s tried to capture move-ment in their canvases. As a further ex-tension of this idea, the partners' latest experiments in design technique involves the translation of their own body lan-guage expressions into tangible architec-tural forms.

With that background in mind, their often complex visual compositions are more easily understandable. Although they had designed smaller and simpler sites such as store facades and an artist's studio in the 1980s, some of their recent executed projects from 1987 to 1989 best exemplify their continuing interest in the complexity of space penetrated by structure caught in motion. The first is a 1987-88 rooftop addition for offices and a conference room of a law firm. Its ab-stracted, bird-like shape, precariously perched atop one of Vienna's classical buildings, was intended to be a new in-terpretation of the numerous late nine-teenth century cupolas atop buildings in that city. Coop Himmelblau's successful competitive design of 1987 to remodel Vienna's Ronacher Theater creates a comparable new roof and internal space atop a nineteenth century building. Their 1988-89 paper factory for the Funder company near St. Veit, near Domenig's slightly earlier information center for the same concern, takes a rec-tangular factory space and dematerialized aspects of it for the conference room and entry door. In both conference spaces, the image of a continuous structural member in what they term a "taut arc" penetrates the space and acts as its spine. Their very latest designs continue these experiments with space, structure, and time. Three new projects designed in 1990, two of them in Europe and one in the United States, deserve mention here.

The first is the Gartenhotel Altmannsdorf in Vienna, whose cantilevered steel structure is somewhat skewed, and whose horizontal roof and floor planes disconcertingly converge. The next even more complex project is handled from their Los Angeles office which they established in 1987 after receiving a commission to design a house in Malibu. Melrose I is a multi-use commercial project which, as with Frank Gehry projects, fits well within the contextless cityscape of Los Angeles. It defines its own context. The planning for a restaurant, vertically moving bar, boutiques, and a bookshop consciously avoids creating individual boxes to suit the various functions. Rather, it is intended to be a complexly designed unit of interrelated spaces which will be subdivided later, depending upon assigned functions. Their newest work in late 1990 and early 1991 being planned is a massive 250,000 square foot home and studio for the German artist Anselm Kiefer, enormous in scale to house his monumental canvases.

Of the five firms that we have seen, the design of Coop Himmelblau may seem to be completely unrelated to the work of the other four. But their interest in the psychological basis of their art has parallels in the earlier development of modernism, and their own structural vocabulary, stripped of ornament, has its roots in the modern movement. Although their work has no overt visual ties to Austria's past, it is Austria's and, particularly, Vienna's unconscious psychological soul that drives their increasingly complex experiments with space, structure, and time.

Conclusion. Or Is It?

Those five architectural firms have neither the contextual cohesion of the New York Five nor the Chicago Seven, or even the cliché film heroes of the *Magnificent Seven.* But those five firms are, in some ways, cowboys in a world of conformists – pioneering individualists who have put Austria on the architectural map of today's world. They are the dynamic, creative forces that their nation lacked in the 1920s and 30s. If architecture is indeed the proverbial mirror of society, then the work of these five architects is tangible proof of the success of Austria's democracy over the past three decades and more. One wonders if Austrian architects now in their twenties and thirties will have the courage to tackle their heritage the way these five have done to move well beyond the images of Secession and Salzburg alike into several different yet complex forms of expression. Only time will tell. We shall all watch more closely as the region and its architecture become the center of world attention in 1995 with the forthcoming World's Fair that will join, in urban celebration, both Vienna and Budapest in a post Cold War reunification of sorts. With the forthcoming end of the millenium, can another Secessionist movement be just around the corner? Or will the continuing complexities of increasingly internationalized Austrian society manifest themselves in another type of spatial movement? Whatever the future has to hold, the undeniable impact of those five firms will have to be acknowledged by their successors.

Ian Wardropper
Austrian Design Today

Design overflows the categories devised to confine it. An activity which encompasses interior and exterior space, functional objects within these spaces, directional signs, and fashion and jewelry worn by the inhabitants defies concise description. Moreover, process and theory have increasingly influential roles in the making of a product. These complexities were acknowledged in the German-speaking world when the English term "design" was adopted in preference to "Formgebung" in the 1950s. The use of the term design indicated recognition of the increasing internationalism of the discipline and that designers were engaging with the broadest dimensions of their profession.

Because of this enlarged context Austrian design cannot be represented as narrowly as Austrian architecture. For the purposes of this exhibition we have chosen to engage four aspects of design: architects' projects outside of building, furniture, jewelry, and industrial design. Hans Hollein and Coop Himmelblau represent the design concerns of architects independent of building; three young design firms, Werner Schmidt, Michael Wagner, and B.R.A.N.D., display aspects of furniture design; Fritz Maierhofer and Gert Mosettig indicate different trends in jewelry; and finally Porsche Design and AVI stand for fundamentally different approaches to industrial design. In highlighting issues of construction, material, and theory these categories de-monstrate the overlap of architectural and design concerns. Selections were made from work which engages in a dialogue with tradition while seeking to move beyond established forms. Finally, the emphasis here is on design which is in production.

History, Geography, Economy

Contemporary Austrian design is clearly linked with the past. The potency today of historical work is remarkable. Clearly the catalytic function of Austrian design of the nineteenth and early twentieth centuries in the formation of modernism and its still-fresh appeal earns the respect of practitioners in the 1990s.

An earlier tradition which still has currency today is the Biedermeier period of about 1815 to 1845. Its reductive force, visible in a chairback or riveting the springing tension of a Dannhauser-designed table at a single joint, certainly embodies a proto-modern spirit. Evolving from the Empire style, Biedermeier's emphasis on comfort expressed the domestic values of the middle classes. And it permitted a new license in furniture-making. Forms could be eccentric and whimsical – reducing a chairback to the silhouette of a plume and playing warm wood tones off electric upholstery colors. This inventive spirit was bolstered by an analytical approach that continues to be a strong factor of Austrian design even today.

Biedermeier currently enjoys a popular revival in America and elsewhere, fur-

1. Michael Thonet, Chaise longue, 1860. Manufactured by Gebrüder Thonet, Vienna and Moravia. Bentwood and caning. (Restricted gift of Mrs. Samuel G. Rautbord to The Art Institute of Chicago, 1970.29)

2. Josef Dannhauser, Side chair, 1815-20. Walnut and walnut veneer. (Gift of The Antiquarian Society from the Capital Campaign Fund to The Art Institute of Chicago, 1987.215.4)

nishing tasteful accents to interior schemes, and on a more theoretical level, serving as a model of recycled classicism for post-modern architects. In Austria, of course, current opinion is more complex; this "dead" style is the subject of renewed respect after decades of serving to symbolize out-moded taste or nostalgia for the past. When Hollein appropriates a Biedermeier form for a chair or a building, his act of borrowing imbues his work with critical associations.

A second design tradition, originating in the 1840s, the radical manufacture and production systems of Thonet, is ingrained in the Austrian mentality. Although conceived in Germany and mainly produced in Moravia and other Austro-Hungarian lands, Thonet furniture was born in Vienna and continues to be associated with the Austrian capital. Michael Thonet (1796-1871) was a carpenter whose new ideas led to his transformation from craftsman to de-

signer. His invention – a process of steam-bending wood – produced light yet sturdy forms. A new repertoire of organic shapes streamed from the firm as manufacturing experiments and expanding markets encouraged variety. Easy assembly and reduction to the fewest functional parts revolutionized furniture production. Honesty, simplicity, and functionality were promoted by Thonet and following Austrian competitors like Jakob and Josef Kohn. These are the same values which so appealed to such later generations as the Kunstreform of the 1890s in the work of Josef Hoffmann and others or the modernist movement of the 1920s and 30s as in the work of Le Corbusier. Thonet Austria today, in trying to keep up to date, produces heavier structures covered with fabrics adapted from the Wiener Werkstätte. The elegant simplicity of structure is in danger of being lost in self-parody. Yet Thonet continues to experiment: Matteo

3. Matteo Thun, Seasonal Chairs, 1989. Manufactured by Thonet Austria. Tubular steel and fabric. (Photo: Studio Azzurro)

Thun's designs of 1989 for seasonal "clothes" for comparable chairs are in the spirit of the firm's original inventiveness and flexibility.

Surprisingly nineteenth century Thonet exerts a stronger influence today than the firm's contemporary designs. The close relationship of designer to manufacturer and continuing interest in lightweight interchangeable or moving parts remain important values. For example, the designers of B.R.A.N.D. worked in steel-bending factories, and their chairs are conceived within the limits of what they know to be the tolerances of their material. Michael Wagner's "Sit-Down" is a flat sheet of metal, cut and folded inward like origami to achieve tensile strength. These designers use metal instead of the bentwood for which Thonet originally became renowned, but then Thonet also pioneered tubular steel construction. In some ways what appears revolutionary in these designs is simply

a reutilisation of Thonet's earlier ideas within a new idiom and exploiting new technologies to make them relevant to today's needs.

Above all the great early modernist tradition of the Wiener Werkstätte period resonates in Austrian design today. Brilliant concepts by Josef Hoffmann, Otto Wagner, and Adolf Loos were given form by skilled craftsmen in small workshops in the first decades of the twentieth century. A Hoffmann-designed chair like the "Sitz-Maschine" brought rectilinear clarity and bold use of geometric motifs to modern chair design. His knowing simplicity and sensuous exposition of wood is as striking now as when it was originally created. Wagner's post office or U-Bahn stations or Olbrich's Secession building are stunning works which still define Viennese urbanity. Wagner's post office is particularly relevant to much contemporary design. His frank exposition of structure to the point of

4. B.R.A.N.D., Armchair "Cosmo ST", 1988. Tubular steel and vinyl. (Photo: Jo Pesendorfer)
5. Michael Wagner, Stool "Sit down", 1984.

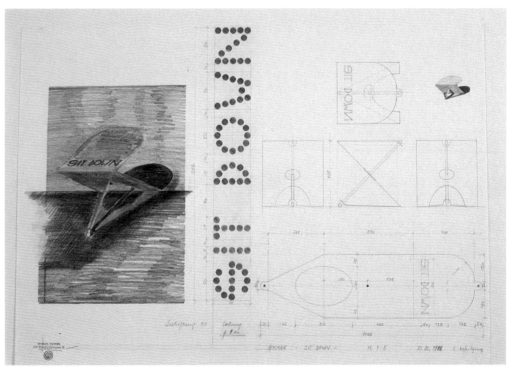

6. Josef Hoffmann, Armchair "Sitzmaschine", c. 1908. Manufactured by Josef and Jakob Kohn, Vienna. Beechwood. (Gift of René Harth Thompson in memory of her father, Charles John Harth, to The Art Institute of Chicago, 1971.743)

making ornament appear functional, his precision and uncompromising geometry yet uncannily sensuous surfaces, his obsession that every detail contribute to the design aesthetic of the whole are values keenly felt today. Mother-of-pearl circles punctuating walnut arms or brass sabots clipping the legs of his 1898-99 armchair illustrate his use of detail.

The events around the Second World War shattered the continuity of Austrian design. Between the time of the Anschluss in 1938, when industry oriented toward warfare, and the postwar recovery, a gap opened in Austrian design history. In the 1930s talented designers like Friedrich Kiesler, proponent of biomorphic forms, emigrated to New York. For those who remained in Austria or southern Germany energy and talent were invested in designing machinery and forms of transportation, such as the Volkswagen, invented in Stuttgart in 1936 by Ferdinand Porsche, father of the present director of Porsche Design; this famous car was manufactured in northern Germany at Wolfsburg. The war eclipsed all non-essential needs and eventually destroyed much of the manufacturing base of the country. As Austria slowly rebuilt in the 1950s, some talented designers such as Oswald Haerdtl and Carl Auböck succeeded in producing tableware and household furnishings which were well suited to the contemporary needs and aesthetic, and acknowledged to some degree earlier achievements in Austrian design by thirties designers such as Josef Hoffmann and Josef Frank. The 1960s released a pent-up well of creativity and fantasy ranging from Christian Ludwig Attersee's surreal tableware to inflatable architecture. In recent decades the design classes at the academies, not only in Vienna but in Linz and Graz, have built up impressive achievements and are setting up new traditions. This break in recent tradition

from the thirties through the fifties helps to explain why contemporary designers are prone to long backward looks towards Biedermeier, Thonet, and the Wiener Werkstätte.

Geography links with history as a critical factor in Austrian design. As a result of its position at the center of the Austro-Hungarian Empire, Vienna attracted talented architects and designers from Czechoslovakia, Yugoslavia, Italy, and southern Germany. The designer-architects of the turn-of-the-century Wiener Werkstätte, including Josef Hoffmann and Joseph Maria Olbrich, came from Moravia and Silesia. Today the boundaries defining the Austrian spirit are equally elastic. For instance, Matteo Thun, born on the Austrian border and trained in Vienna, now lives mostly in Milan and practices for Italian industry. He still teaches in Vienna, but represented Italy at a recent design conference. Practice in Austria is the guideline here.

Austria's small size and dependence on export markets has a significant impact on its design. A limited market within Austria forces designers either to restrain their ambitions to a small production or to orient themselves towards their country's principal neighbors and trading partners, Germany and Italy. If success is measured in volume and broad distribution, then Porsche Design has clearly overcome the limits of geography. From its mountain redout at Zell-am-See it sends designs to clients throughout Europe, and beyond to Japan and America; production takes place around the world. Its designs are clearly recognizable yet also universal and contemporary in tone.

Small-scale production can be turned into a positive value. Critic and historian François Burkhardt, for example, believes in individual consumer choice and in diversity over uniformity ("Tendencies in German Design Theories in the past Fifteen Years," in Victor Margolin (ed.), *Design Discourse,* 1989, pp. 49-54). Small production operations can be more responsive to individual needs and more innovative than larger concerns. Economically, too, the fragmentation of the consumer market has encouraged smaller operations, which can update products more quickly. In 1984 designer Charlotte Perriand stated: "I think we can anticipate a return to a more primitive form of craftsmanship – not in the sense of going back to the techniques of the past, but a return to smaller scales of operations…" In this light Austria's limitations could lead to creative solutions to design problems. As long as the distribution networks can be properly established, good designs from a small country such as Austria can fulfill consumer needs elsewhere. Looked at in another way, regionalism can be enlisted in the fight against the sterility of much post-modern design and architecture, as Kenneth Frampton argues in "Place-form and Cultural Identity," in John Thackara (ed.), *Design After Modernism,* 1988, pp. 51-66. Rather than identifying local traditions as provincial in a pejorative sense, the firmly rooted qualities of a small country can be positive. The rich matrix of local cultural traditions can serve as a source of forms to counter the bland proliferations of "Euro-design".

This leads to the charged question, "What characterizes Austrian design?" It is tempting, if dangerous, to compare Austria to its neighbors, because German and Italian design are more clearly defined in the popular mind. The German is rational and well-behaved; the Italian is stylish and emotional. German design is rectangular and reliable, with utility predominating. In Italy, aestheticism rules; the designer is given more freedom to create and artisanry is preserved. Austria certainly exhibits some characteristics of these neighbors. Precision as well as style characterizes its design. German intensity is softened by an Italian sense of relaxation. These traits can be observed in works as disparate as Mosettig's precisely milled metal fabrications which often surprise the wearer to Michael Wagner's sharp-edged phone table with its playful anthropomorphic shape.

Self-analysis – borrowing a term from native son Sigmund Freud – is an essential trait of Austrian design. Rigorous scrutiny to gauge the appropriateness of form to function, and even to search for inner qualities, is part of the design process in Vienna. The psychoanalyst's couch is always ready, the patient always questioning himself. The result is a healthy clarification and also a liberating appreciation of the sensual and fantastic realms. At its best Austrian design has emotional appeal while maintaining flawless technical control.

Obsession with detail is a by-product of this analytical tendency. In contemporary design the rivets on Schmidt's folding table, Hollein's crisp bronze lyre on the Bösendorfer piano, the hinges on Mosettig's jewelry are elevated from minor notes to major themes. This same tendency can be traced across the terrain of historical Austrian design. The proliferation of mounts on Biedermeier furniture, the perfect curve of a bentwood chair, the small wooden spheres which punctuate Josef Hoffmann's "Seven Bullet" chair are all elements which signal an extraordinary attention to detail.

Finally, there is a quality of reticence or shyness in Austrian design. Against the plain-spoken, out-going ways of American society this discretion is particularly noticeable; for the most part, these works eschew color or dramatic form in favor of quiet elegance. Even Hollein's piano, at first sight the perfect instrument for Liberace, is not as loud as its parts would make it appear. A becoming modesty and quiet sense of quality are the best part of this virtue.

This brief survey focusses only on a portion of Austrian design. There is much interesting work that has been left out. With the emphasis here on production design, an important area which crosses boundaries between art and design is not included. Franz West's chairs, swooping in expansive gestures or cradling newspapers in racks of rough steel, warp concepts of function and plumb the emotional depths of these seemingly ordinary objects. But arresting as this work is, it is primarily exhibited and perceived as sculpture in art galleries. Wolfgang Podgorschek's chairs and tables fabricated from cereal and spaghetti packages play with notions of a consumer society and our current obsession with recycling; but his deliberately flimsy objects are philosophical manifestations of Platonic ideas rather than solid reality. Heinz Frank currently designs objects which are anthropomorphic, playful creatures which we might call naive art were they not labelled design. All of this work of a speculative and whimsical nature is, it seems to us, very Austrian and in a larger sense represents a movement in international design to expand beyond the strictures of mass production.

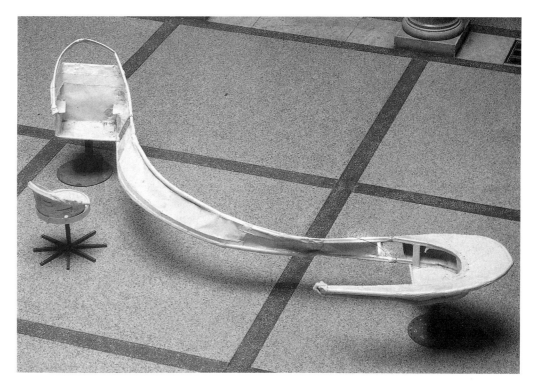

8. Franz West, "Eo ipso", 1987. Lacquered iron in two parts. (Museum für angewandte Kunst, Vienna, Inv. Nr. GK 10)

But we have chosen to limit this showing to tangible products.

Interior design, while bearing directly on our basic concerns, is not represented in this exhibition. Inseparable from architecture on the one hand and furniture design on the other, interior design occupies an area between the two. Particularly in Vienna, this activity is often the stimulus to furniture design in cafes, restaurants, and shops. As theatres of society and showplaces for consumer goods, these contexts encourage flights of creativity. Austrian architects and designers have responded dramatically to the challenge of these sites for commerce and commingling. The recent restoration of the Loos Bar signalled the influence of this early twentieth-century interior on design of our times. Mirrored surfaces visually expand its tiny four-table seating area and dissolve the precise geometry of wall panels and ceiling into a place for reveries and late-night dreams. Loos' ability to use materials which create an intensely emotional setting and his sensuous geometry – down to the tactile sensation of holding his grid-cut Lobmeyr glasses – is admired today. The irony is that Loos, forever associated with the statement "Ornament is a crime" has become a father to the symbol-crazy post-modern generation. Hollein's own early shops and travel agencies reflect Loos' precise, jewel-like surfaces at the same time that they introduced such representational devices as palm trees and pyramids, which became his most famous contribution to design.

In the 1960s and 70s other Austrian designers shared Loos' astonishing combination of purity and theatricality in the creation of their interiors. Jiszda's Henn store (1973) with its pulverized marble surface interior created a pure space as dream-like as an ideal city. Much of his later work, especially trade exhibits for Sony, Wega, and in America for Apple Computers, used minimal structures of fabric suspended from a spider's web of wires to create expansive environments within clean structural lines.

Recent interior spaces created by designers continue these efforts to use bars and restaurants as laboratories for design ideas. These range from Eichinger oder Knechtl's cool and understated Café Wrenkh to B.R.A.N.D.'s caverns of connected rods or raw Black Market Bar to Arno Grünberger's Café Concert definition of space and emotional response by color. Such spaces are self-conscious and overtly stylish; they intend to elicit an emotional response; and they insist on absolute integration of furnishings with decor. Many furnishings, such as B.R.A.N.D.'s bookshelves, can be produced and used independently of their environment but were nonetheless born from these larger systems and respond to a specific interior. Other cities teem with short-lived restaurants featuring the latest designs; but it is clear that in a cafe society like Vienna, these institutions play a special role in encouraging and disseminating design. While the areas of art/design and interior design may be missing from the exhibition, they are certainly a background to the

9-12. Matthäus Jiszda, Henn store, Vienna, 1973.
13,14. B.R.A.N.D., Black Market bar and shop, Gonzagagasse 9, Vienna, 1989-90.

work. Other areas of design, such as textiles, ceramics, and graphics, are certainly active in Austria today, but were not as sharply defined and clearly tied to the themes of structural relationships between buildings and objects which we are trying to capture in the exhibition and book.

Architects Design

A notable feature of 1980s design was the adulation of architects; these culture heroes were allowed numerous opportunities to create objects other than buildings. Department store displays offered a sumptuous array of Swid Powell dinner plates by Michael Graves or Stanley Tigerman, Alessi silver tea services by Aldo Rossi or Hans Hollein. This phenomenon, which had begun by the mid-seventies, was prompted by the lack of building opportunities in a recession; the theoretical orientation of post-modernism also encouraged architects to draw and exhibit more frequently. Even dead architects benefited from this trend posthumously. Prices for Frank Lloyd Wright chairs and stained glass windows reached new heights at auction; modernist reproductions seemed to be everywhere. This trend is inevitably associated with the excesses of Reagan's America and a similarly affluent Europe. It led to the creation of many superfluous objects but undeniably invigorated the design scene. Although Hans Hollein's works could easily be classified among celebrity architect's designs, such a label would underrate his importance in the field and the critical role of design in his career.

Hollein's searching approach to design was evident in the 1970s, when at the Venice Biennale he exhibited a half racing car/half object, which dissociated form and function and questioned the very nature of design. In America his ideas became known through a noted exhibition "Man transFORMS", which he was commissioned to organize as the inaugural show for the Cooper-Hewitt Museum, The Smithsonian Institution's National Museum of Design, in 1976. Through participatory events, including city walking tours, the exhibition provoked speculation about the physical and metaphysical range of design issues. In addition to analyzing the philosophical nature of design, Hollein began producing objects, particularly furniture. While this was necessary to supplement earnings from the meagre architectural commissions then available to him in Austria, Hollein was also demonstrating his allegiance to an Austrian tradition. Many Wiener Werkstätten designers – Josef Hoffmann, Otto Wagner, Adolf Loos – were principally architects; in some cases, most notably Hoffmann's, the designs now overshadow the architecture.

Hollein's early designs have a strong pop flavor: a dressing table, "Marilyn", features pink plumage framing a semicircular mirror and summons the glitz and showmanship of Hollywood. As the only Austrian associated with the predominantly Italian design group Memphis, he essayed a number of post-modern furnishings in the early 1980s. In what Michael Collins terms the "dragnet" approach of post-modernism, Hollein snared various sources in his designs. "Schwarzenberg", a briar wood table of 1981 combines a stepped Art Deco-inspired top with a modernist design – so open and delicately balanced that it is positively flimsy. Since the 1980s Hollein has been closely associated with post-modernism. At its best post-modernism embraces pluralism over uniformity and champions the artistic over the functional. Past modes are redesigned to respond to present

15. Hans Hollein, Aircraft-carrier-city in landscape, 1963. Collage.

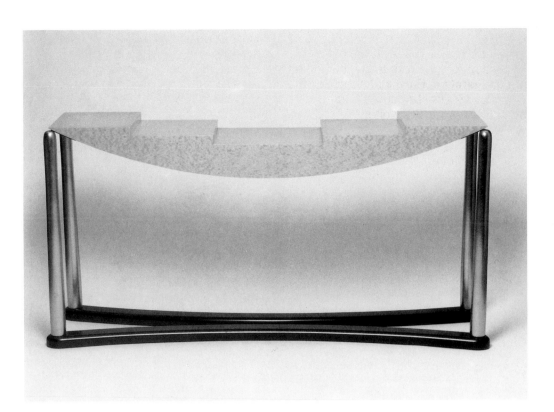

attitudes. On the negative side postmodernism often descends into vapid eclecticism, permits shoddy workmanship in the name of artistic license, and becomes too obviously linked with the lifestyle of a prosperous decade.

Hollein's voice in the dialogue of postmodernism is laden with irony and symbolism. One of his most successful designs was the tea and coffee service for Alessi in 1983. Adventurously, the Italian production company invited architects from several countries to design silver services. While most of the submissions resemble miniature houses, Hollein's looks like an aircraft carrier; criss-crossing runways form the tray and needle-nose spouted pitchers prepare for sorties to replenish empty cups. The design's success owes to the appropriateness of the symbolism, the intuitive leap to the conclusion that a tea service is more like an aircraft carrier than a house: it moves wherever needed, its vessels are in constant motion filling cups and returning to the tray. At the same time the connotations of war are ironical, far from the domestic tranquility of teatime. In a 1963 work on paper Hollein employed the image of an aircraft carrier, collaging one over a photograph of a rolling landscape. It was a part of his exploration of form and symbolism in architecture, which later found palpable form in silver. Hollein's symbolic use of giant structures on a small scale is employed not only in the Alessi tea and coffee set but also in other tableware. Turreted monuments turned into silver centerpieces for Rossi and Arcandi or glass bowls and candleholders for Cleto Munari are solid designs but do not stir the imagination as much as the earlier tea service.

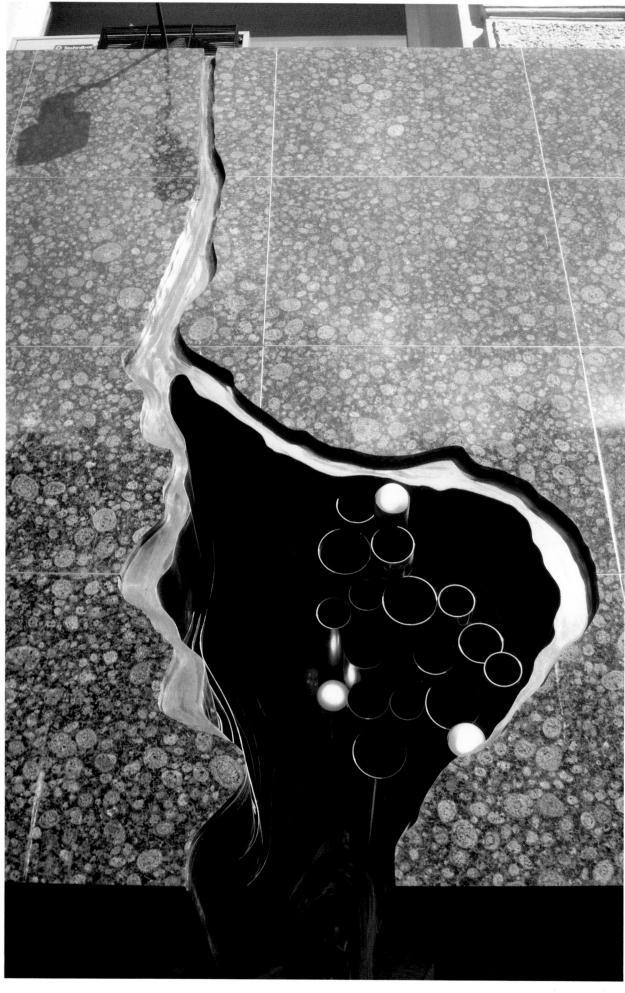

One of Hollein's most recent designs, the Bösendorfer grand piano, is a fascinating study in tradition and innovation. For over a century and a half this firm has constructed pianos in the music-loving capital of Vienna, often inviting well-known artists, architects, and designers to draw up plans for showpiece pianos. Hans Makart's 1867 piano for Empress Eugénie of France, supported by a lavish gilded base charged with lyre-playing youths, was perfectly in tune with the opulent Second Empire. The rippling wood surface of Josef Hoffmann's instrument emphasized the craftsmanship of the Wiener Werkstätte in 1909; Norbert Schlesinger's 1958 piano is a sculptural statement of period design, a play of organic curves against blunt edges.

Hollein's piano acknowledges these earlier examples: its shiny brass legs and lush red lacquered interior has the flamboyance of Makart and some of the sculptural quality of Schlesinger. But his own re-reading of the form is obvious in the dissociation of the parts. He emphasizes the structural nature of the legs and lyre which with their angled form are clearly distinct from the traditional body of the piano. Hollein has rethought the piano design architecturally: the legs are

shaped like I-beams; the piano lid has an all-over, seemingly random, design like his ceiling in the Haas-Haus; the sheet music support bears a zigzag opening, which is a kind of signature motif on some of his buildings. These red, black, white, and gold elements are chromatically unified but the piano elements are deliberately left in a tense relationship.

While product design has been an integral part of Hollein's career since the beginning, Coop Himmelblau has turned to this activity only during the past year. Their armchair "Vodöl" for Vitra, marking their departure from pure building design, is a deconstruction of a classic architect's chair design of 1928-29, Le Corbusier's "LC2 Armchair". Wolf Prix and Helmut Swiczinsky begin with the same elements as the French modernist – polished tubing supporting an upholstered cube – but they unravel the composition and introduce a problematic new feature, a slanted I-beam. This I-beam, intruding like the Rhinoceros in an Ionesco play, tilts the cube back so that the tubing now wraps around and counterbalances it and the seat cushions are cut at a bias to remain parallel to the ground. Like their buildings, the out-of-kilter elements of the chair require

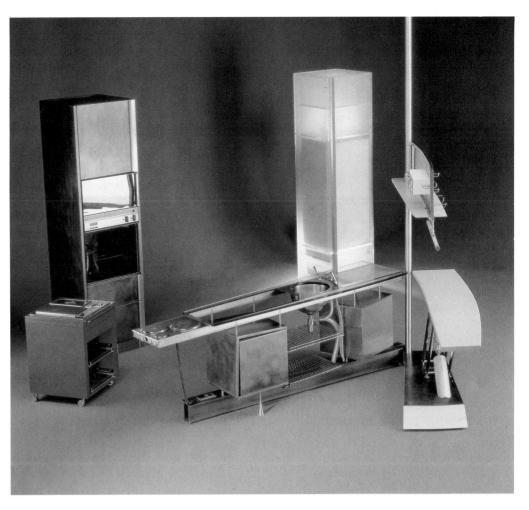

meticulous planning. Poised between whimsy and aggression, the chair challenges its surroundings, deliberately occupying more space than it should. It asks questions: How to sit safely without tripping? How to fit it into a conventional decor?

There is an Alice-through-the-looking-glass quality to much Coop Himmelblau work that forces one to question preconceptions of buildings and furniture and establishes an alternate but wholly convincing order. Their recent kitchen design indicates that the firm is increasingly interested in the question of how to extend their architectural thinking to product design and how to concentrate their radical spatial rethinking to smaller units.

Three Furniture Designers

Austria has a long history of innovation in furniture design; there are a number of practitioners of this field who bring an inventive excitement to their designs. Werner Schmidt folds or rolls his furniture. "Klapptisch" has the elegant economy of a mathematical equation. Eight sections of a circle hinge to each other and to rectangular supports. Made from

aluminium, an important national product of Austria, the material is light enough to fold as easily as a fan. But this durable metal, associated with industry and aerospace, also has great tensile strength. The ingenuity of the design and its limitless conformations from closed to extended make this table intellectually satisfying and visually provocative. Folding tables are a traditional furniture form from occasional card tables to fire screens. Yet Schmidt has focussed on the process of folding as the subject rather than as an element of structure. Visually, the absolute geometry of the table is softened by the dull shine of aluminium and enlivened by the spiky texture of the rivets adorning its surface.

Schmidt has thoroughly explored the principles of folding in other work as well. A geometrical series of primary colored chairs – circle, square, triangle – extends this theme. A logical and playful corollary of these ideas is the chair which folds from flat to open in the shape of jig-saw puzzle pieces. Schmidt has also designed a lamp for Woka consisting of eight illuminated panels which can be bent into an infinite variety of lighted shapes. These adaptable, compact objects are practical but also emo-

19. Hans Hollein, Grand Piano, 1990. Manufactured by Bösendorfer, Vienna. (Photo: Dr. Parisini)
20. Hans Makart, Grand Piano for Empress Eugenie of France, 1867. Manufactured by Bösendorfer, Vienna.
21. Norbert Schlesinger, Grand Piano, 1958. Manufactured by Bösendorfer, Vienna.
22. Coop Himmelblau, Kitchen, 1990. Manufactured by EWE. Steel and stainless steel. (Photo: Josef Hoflehner)

tionally satisfying in that they invite the user to participate in the design solutions.

Schmidt is interested in other applications of folding. The "Rolladen-Stuhl" uses wooden Venetian blinds to make a collapsible, portable chair. Both the variety of shapes and the surprising use of a familiar material make this chair appealing. One of his most recent designs is a picnic hamper designed from the inside out instead of outside in. Based on traditional Alpine egg carriers, he has designed compartments for individual items of a meal, which when closed create mysteriously shaped objects. The more enigmatic side of the designer's work, contrasting with his clear geometry, can be seen in a six-sided wooden stool, each side with a different texture, presumably offering a variety of experiences to the sitter.

Having studied with Hans Hollein at the Hochschule für angewandte Kunst,

Schmidt is an architect as well as designer. A 1985 project for a moveable bridge, the Ponte dell'Accademia in Venice, indicates that his interest in flexible objects extends to larger structures, too. His work clearly revolves around structural principles which make his objects practical, yet give aesthetic choices to their owners in the process of their use. His production is small, his activity akin to an inventor's, experimenting and tinkering with ideas. His work could sustain far greater production. Only several dozen of the "Klapptisch", for example, have been produced, and yet it is clearly designed for mass-production and could sustain wider distribution.

Another designer who makes good use of folded metal is Michael Wagner. Unlike Schmidt's, his works typically are folded rather than folding, that is, cut from a single sheet of metal and bent permanently into position. His "Sit-Down" stool, for instance, makes eco-

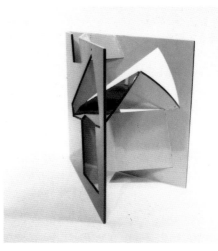

nomical use of a thin metal sheet folded and secured for flexible, tensile strength, but is not intended to open and shut. Interested in simplicity of production, Wagner has produced under Edition W a line of related designs: a drinks trolley, telephone stand, wardrobe, shelving unit – which with their faintly anthropomorphic stances seem to be members of the same race. Of perforated silver metal they are modest objects which obligingly perform simple tasks with the character of cartoon stick-figures. They are also deliberately mobile furniture, ready to be wheeled into use as the changing demands of a day require.

Wagner's minimalist but evocative forms translate into wood and glass as well as metal. He also produces wood furniture on stands of spindly triangular legs; their gangly height makes one title, "Giraffe", particularly apt. He is also capable of designing subtly stylish bespoke furniture with a sophisticatedly Viennese flair. Like Schmidt, he, too, has a penchant for bulging, enigmatic forms, visible in the glass vase table of triple inverted cones fused into a table top, produced for a competition named Liberta.

The design duo B.R.A.N.D. provides a third example of the successful exploitation of metal for furniture. During their formative period this pair completely avoided the academic establishment in Vienna, developing their orientation towards design while working in metal-bending factories. The designers are also workers; they make their own products. At the heart of their creation lies a re-spect for the physical limitations of bending metal and of manual labor. First impressions of their work give the sense of "fifties revival"; but while there may be an historicist element, their consistent exploration of curving metal in all dimensions transcends this label.

Stepping into one of their environments is like entering a grotto: it has the ability to transform a space without obscuring or physically connecting to it. One of their designs, "Raumdezvous", for a now-defunct bar, depends on a system of interconnected flexible metal rods from which bookcases and lighting fixtures are suspended within a total environment. In developing this system they adapted it to occupy any space. Some chairs, desks, and other furniture in this tubular style have been designed for specific commissions. Bookcases have the delicacy of Art Nouveau; they span a room like a spider's web yet bear surprisingly heavy loads. Theatrical, and perhaps as temporary as stage sets, B.R.A.N.D.'s infinitely expandable system has the possibility of fulfilling a need and supplying a mood almost instantaneously.

A series of curved metal chairs inevitably invites comparison with Thonet. The design duo tend to reduce their forms to carefully defined arcs covered with stretched vinyl, which push to the edge of practicality. Their circular "Cosmo" bookcase is a wholly satisfying design: a system of moveable supports allows the user to tailor a configuration of shelves to his needs, creating at the same time a very strong linear pattern

29. Fritz Maierhofer, Brooch, 1974. Gold and acrylic. (Private collection)
30. Fritz Maierhofer, Brooch, 1986-87. Oxidized white metal and yellow metal. (Private collection)

against the circular structure. With a circumference gauged to the extention of a person's limbs this bookcase can be set against the wall or wheeled into use as a room-divider. Like Schmidt and Wagner, B.R.A.N.D. consistently analyses and explores an idea through its logical permutations.

These three design firms tend to emphasize flexibility through folding or manipulating materials. Much of their work is made of metal, intended to be economical, and aimed at mass-production. There are many other Austrian designers of furniture, though mainly this is an area of individual commissions (bespoke furniture). These range from the elegant, sophisticated design practiced by Hermann Czech – one of the ablest restaurant designers in Vienna – or the chic work of Luigi Blau, to the bulbous forms of Oswald Oberhuber, mainly, though not exclusively working in wood. We have decided instead to look at some younger designers, working principally in metal who are trying, against the odds, to go into production. But these designers represent only one tendency in Austrian design today.

Jewelry

Jewelry is an art form which skirts the edges of design. More associated with craftsmanship of individual pieces and therefore resembling the fine arts, this art form can of course be produced in editions. Jewelry can be simply a fashionable adornment; it can also approach conceptual art, as does the work of Munich goldsmith Otto Künzli. In the last couple of decades jewelry's range has expanded beyond mere personal adornment, increasingly probing the boundaries of expectations. In Austria jewelry and jewelry-making are weighty with tradition. Under successive emperors goldsmithery and gem-cutting reached levels of staggering virtuosity. Today a visit to the Schatzkammer leaves an indelible impression of the sumptuous tastes of the Habsburgs. More recently architects and designers of the Wiener Werkstätte turned their talents towards body ornaments as well as household furnishings, mixing the dazzling surface pattern of Gustav Klimt and other Secession painters with a more modern sensibility.

Austrian jewelry today swings between the poles of ornament and structural simplicity. In the sixties and seventies

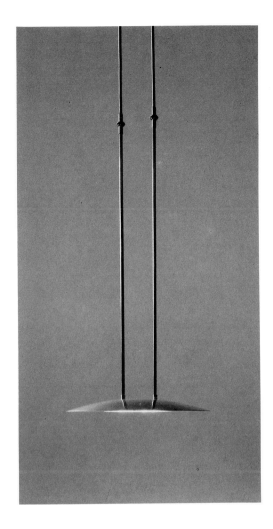

31. Gert Mosettig, Hanging lamp, 1990. Brass.

an important exhibition site in Vienna, Galerie Am Graben, encouraged a new generation of jewelers, two of whom, Fritz Maierhofer and Gert Mosettig, make for interesting comparisons.

Maierhofer began exhibiting in 1971. The precision and technical command of his early pieces reflected the considerable experience gained in the jewelry firm Anton Heldwein and in supervising the Omega watch collection production. Works from the 1970s reveal two of his preoccupations: structure resonant of architecture and the mixing of fine with "base" materials. An early brooch from 1974 consists of gold riveted together like sheets of metal; within a semi-circular opening at its base spokes radiate outwards like industrial machinery over a wavy rainbow of acrylics. Though it is a small piece (9 x 9 cm.), its internal scale suggests a building facade. And the inclusion of plastic gives a colorful pop art jolt to the luxury material. Maierhofer has explored these themes over the past two decades. After experiments with the hardness of steel and the softness of tin, he returned to his initial interests in expressing architectural structure through precious materials. As a research fellow at the Sir John Cass Faculty of Art, London, in 1987, Maierhofer completed an internally consistent body of work which was exhibited at the Victoria and Albert Museum. These pieces took the form of miniature girders, fragments seemingly ready to join the skeleton of a building or a bridge. Engineered with absolute precision, these works are sometimes oxidized white metal to suggest weathering, sometimes left in a yellow gold; both materials are often combined for deliberate contrast. Their scale pushes the limit of a wearable brooch, and in fact they demand to be taken as sculpture, up-staging the wearer.

As architectural fragments, these pieces naturally call to mind the deconstructivist buildings of Coop Himmelblau. In fact, they are utterly distinct from the architect's concepts. While at first seeming random or asymmetrical, these gold objects are completely self-contained. Their power and drama come from association with the real world of steel girders and their authoritative technical mastery. But they do not seek to explode accepted notions of structure or to confront us with near-chaotic decomposition. Rather they are rarified, precisely and even inevitably composed works.

Maierhofer's latest work appears to add complexity and luxury to his absolute and minimalist statements. The girders are disappearing, replaced by stiletto-pointed wedges and sometimes encrusted with a regular pattern of jewels. A hint of fin-de-siècle Vienna is creeping into the work, relaxing the severity of the London-period pieces.

If Maierhofer's work is abstract and complete within itself, Mosettig's work is tactile and needs contact with the body to be activated. Even photographs presenting the work reinforce the contrasting approaches; Maierhofer's lie on a neutral ground, Mosettig's on the body of a friend. Maierhofer labors in the isolation of a country farmhouse; Mosettig in the midst of a lively Viennese arts community.

Mosettig works almost exclusively with non-precious metals: steel, brass, sometimes rubber. His work is designed so that it can be produced in limited numbers. While Maierhofer uses traditional goldsmith techniques to create unique jewelry which resembles industrial by-products, Mosettig uses machines and metal-working tools to forge instruments so refined that they become jewelry.

Much of the interest in Mosettig's jewelry lies in the conceptual challenge which it poses to a prospective wearer. Facing two small spheres and a double-hoop, one does not leap to the conclusion that these combine to form a ring. But once the problem is solved, the ring fits on the finger comfortably, rolling with the movements of the hand. A thin flat piece of metal folds open to become a ring. A band of metal surprisingly fits on the finger. Mosettig designs for the body. Uncompromising geometry is cunningly tailored to human needs. Like a magician he delights in pulling objects from his bag of tricks to confound and amaze the viewer.

Maierhofer's and Mosettig's activities outside of jewelry reveal other aspects of their design orientation. Maierhofer has completed a number of large-scale public and private outdoor sculpture; these indicate the degree to which he considers his brooches abstractions independent of the human form. Mosettig has recently constructed a number of lamps or lighting features. Through the use of high-intensity bulbs he is able to reduce his lamps to thin rods or disks which almost disappear in the aura of light which emanates from them. Milled with the same precision as his jewelry, these lighting fixtures float in space. They are the most ethereal of metal forms and merge with space in the same way that his jewelry, seemingly so rigid, adapts to the human form.

Industrial Design

Design for industry numbers few professionals in Austria. Yet there are some exemplary responses to the problems of designing for a country with a small population and manufacturing base. One comes from a design company, Porsche Design, with so distinctive a style that its work is sought out internationally. The other is a manufacturing concern, AVI, that encourages creative uses and designs for its basic product, plastic-coated mesh.

Porsche is a famous design family. Ferdinand (called Ferry) Porsche created the Volkswagen "Beetle"; several decades later his son Ferdinand Alexander Porsche followed with the "911 coupé" which bears his name as well as the "Carrera 904" and the "Targa 911" series. Wishing to expand his range beyond sports cars, Ferdinand Alexander Porsche established his own design firm in 1972 and soon after left his birth-place, Stuttgart, Germany, for Zell am See, Austria, the site of a family estate he had stayed on as a child. Realizing that with today's communications systems international design could be practiced anywhere, Porsche settled in this mountainous locale near Salzburg and gathered a team of designers around him.

Stream-lining and functionalism carried over from car to product design; ski-goggles, watches, pens, brief-cases, lounge chairs were conceived in Zell am See and produced by companies throughout Europe, America and Japan. Clarity of form characterizes all of the work. Basic black is the signature color, a neutral shade which emphasizes shape but also connotes power. Function is foremost and those objects which express this clearly are the most successful. There is also a tendency for these works to become so sculptural that function can appear secondary. An in-

32. Porsche Design, Television set "M55-911", 1989. Designed for Grundig AG.

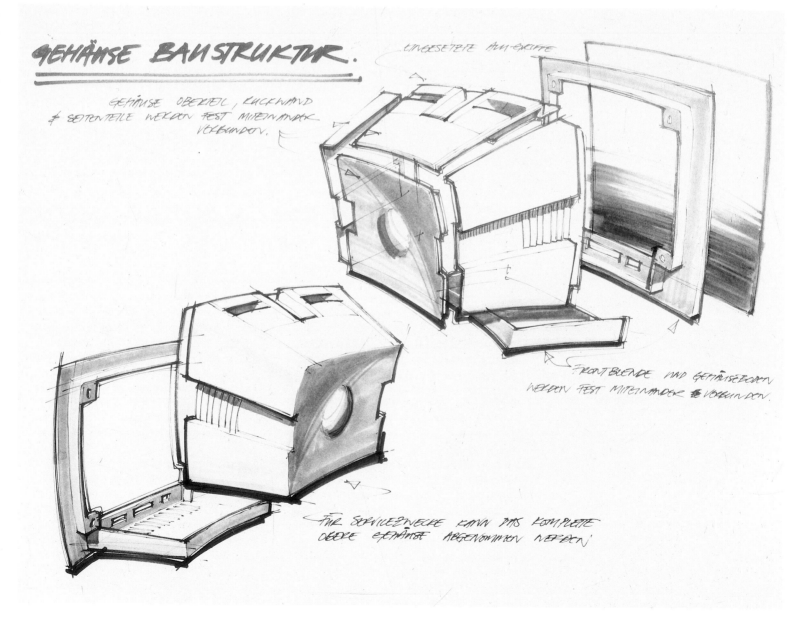

33. Porsche Design, Alternative motorcycle concept, 1984. Full scale model.

novative approach to problem-solving has led to ideas like the slide-rule extension for the PAF lamp or the rotating dial for the telephone, which respond to contemporary needs for compactness and flexibility. The Grundig television set (1989) separates and emphasizes the picture screen. An inward-curving body expresses the idea of rays emanating from a single source. The remote-control unit slips on top like a backpack for use in place as well as removes for controlling from afar. The whole set rotates on a self-pedestal.

Some of the firm's designs offer solutions in advance of perceived need. Their motorcycle stresses comfort (heated handlebars) and safety (covered wheels). These features are not yet demanded by sufficient numbers of motorcyclists to encourage wide production. But Porsche has produced an undeniably powerful concept and image. Porsche designs are sleek, authoritative, stylish and func-

tional in equal measure. Function forces style.

There is an absolutism to Porsche design which is at once the source of its strength and, occasionally, its weakness. The designs are so uncompromising that when successful they seem to be the ultimate conclusion, the clearest and even the only possible solution to a problem. The black exteriors yield no secrets, remaining aloof and exclusive. Yet the powerful and alluring curved forms invite touch. For Porsche, limitations are a springboard to creativity: "Design is the product of a sound appreciation that freedom is never absolute. It is always relative, determined by the purpose and function of an object and restricted by the materials you use." This attitude inevitably leads to problems: the bomb-shaped lighters that are too heavy, children's car seats so sturdy that they are too expensive for most consumers. Despite occasional lapses, Porsche carries design to its logical endpoint with mastery that few can equal.

Porsche Design has no manufacturing capacity and designs on commission. By contrast AVI has a product, welded wire mesh fire-lacquered in hepox-powders. The company sought design innovation to find new applications for its metal work. Founded in the 1950s, AVI has become one of the largest welding-machine companies in the world, producing mesh of various grades, from reinforcement for concrete to fencing to display racks. In the early 1980s one of the company officers, Max Droschl, had the idea of inviting designs, for furniture to be made of the company's industrial material. This is a concept with some history in Austria. At the turn of the century the Wiener Werkstätte turned to "Gitterwerk" – metal trellis work – for inspiration in a number of their products. Josef Hoffmann and Koloman Moser designed silver or silvered brass planters and cruet holders in simple grid patterns that are severely modern. AVI's simple idea is to design geometrical furniture from sheets of mesh; the grid pattern's inherent visual structure gives this furniture immediate clarity.

Droschl designed several chairs and sofas by simply bolting together prefabricated units of square mesh. Absolutely simple and adaptable (the owner could bolt the units together in different configurations) they make a strong visual statement because of the powerful geometrical pattern. The voids of the mesh also have the visual effect of ap-

pearing solid in certain lights and from some viewpoints, so that the furniture varies in visual weight.

Droschl also invited some young designers to draw up plans for furniture. Alexander Korab devised "Chaise Longue Lechos" (1983) in which a continuous sheet of mesh bends back to intersect itself, forming polyhedrons to support a reclining human figure. For comfort, triangular and cylindrical pillows are attached. But the flexible nature of mesh can itself be a factor of comfort. Korab's "Chair Klisia" (1983) flexes slightly when one sits in it, yielding to the weight of the sitter. Finally, the designers Alke John and Fritz Maresch, then teamed as the group IDEEN, began a series of pavilions. These garden follies, roofed but open-walled, come in a variety of styles, echoing the Gothic, Japanese, Renaissance. Like the furniture, the pavilions are pleasingly simple, appropriate to their function, and sufficiently durable to withstand out-door climate and conditions.

The AVI line was perhaps principally conceived as garden furniture, since it cannot be damaged by rain and has no solid parts to collect water. The Austrian climate may not be ideally suited to such furniture, but Italy is both warm and design-conscious, and has provided the market for these furnishings. The main problem is that the mesh seating is too expensive to produce for the mass furniture market. Also metal is not inherently comfortable. AVI still produces some furniture but apparently sees little future for it.

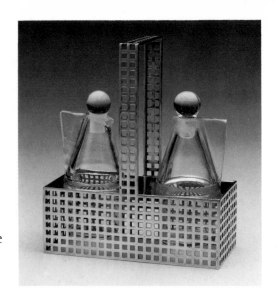

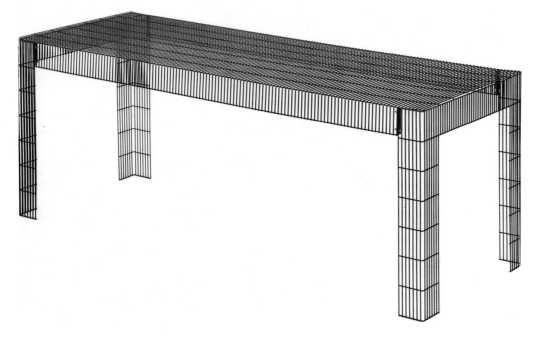

34. Max Droschl, Bench, 1985. Manufactured by AVI, Graz. Welded wire mesh, fire lacquered in hepox-powders.
35. Kolomon Moser, Cruet stand, 1904-05. Manufactured by Alfred Mayer, Wiener Werkstätte. Silver and glass. (Restricted gift of Mrs. Julian Armstrong, Jr., and Mrs. George B. Young to The Art Institute of Chicago, 1987.219-1-3a-b)
36. Ideen, "Pavilion Belvedere", 1982. Manufactured by AVI, Graz. Welded wire mesh and weather resistant cloth. (Photo: Petek)

65

Concluding Thoughts

The designers discussed in this brief report on Austrian design are in no sense a group; in fact, some represent divergent approaches to products. Nor can they stand for the multiplicity of design as practiced in this country today. But they do share some concerns, which are relevant to the state of design today. One is invention, whether formal, such as Schmidt's jig-saw puzzle chair, metaphorical, as in Hollein's tea and coffee service, or technological, like Porsche Design's Grundig television set.

A second principle which has a clear role in Austrian design is flexibility. B.R.A.N.D.'s infinitely changeable tubular systems, AVI's easily assembled mesh furniture, Porsche's telescoping lamp or rotating telephone dial, Schmidt's lightweight, folding tables, Wagner's moveable wardrobes, all offer the consumer choices. As society becomes more complex and less uniform, individuals seek objects which can be tailored to their own use. Folding furnishings have of course always existed. In the Renaissance tables and chairs were often made to be moved since the function of rooms was less rigidly defined and the homeowner wished to change living arrangements at will. The need to adapt living spaces has in some ways returned, and we grow accustomed to more fluid, less fixed situations. Innovation and flexibility, characteristic of Austria since Thonet, are as important today as ever.

What is the future of Austrian design? The recent crumbling of established political orders in Central Europe requires Austria to confront its past as a condition of facing its future. If the political map is to be redrawn, what will Austria's position be? The first Central European Design Conference, convened in Vienna in October 1990, responded to this question; and at its conclusion a declaration was issued recommending cooperation and information sharing. Geographically and politically, Austria is well placed to assist in re-opening the lines of communication among Central European countries. Before launching programs of design reform, many former Eastern Bloc countries need first to reexamine their historical design. Czechoslovakia looks back to legendary designers of the twenties, such Otto Wagner students as Jan Kotera, Josef Gocar, and Pavel Janak, as a means to assess the future. Hungary reviews its engineering feats in locomotives and motorcycles. Poland and Yugoslavia have desperate economic hurdles to clear before they can even proceed. Issues of social justice are pressing, and economy will be a critical factor for countries facing drastic political change. But one key role for the designer is to mediate between industry and society and create economic solutions. It is clear that designers need to be involved more in the industrial process, whether from without as Porsche or from within as AVI. The 1995 Vienna-Budapest World's Fair may be an important occasion to explore the role of design in Europe, particularly Central Europe, just as historically such expositions have launched new products and designs.

If design can improve the quality of life and mediate between man and his technological environment, then it has an increasingly important and difficult role. The mission of design is not limited to the technical and functional. Man has the psychological need for other dimensions in products, including the aesthetic, emotional, and symbolic. Many of the designers discussed here do incorporate metaphor and emotional dimensions in their work and explore new formal attitudes. The need for imagination and innovation in design is constant; at the same time a strong historical tradition, such as can be found in Vienna, can be a wellspring of inspiration. If production and distribution capacities can be harnessed, Austria has an abundance of imaginative and flexible designers to summon forth.

Amy Gold
Illustrated Biographies

The following biographies are alphabetically arranged to avoid any sense of hierarchy. Their purpose is to complement information in the essays by Ian Wardropper and John Zukowsky, in order to convey the general feeling surrounding the Austrian architecture and design community.

The biographies are essentially short résumés, which I feel cover information which is both relevant and comprehensible to novice and expert alike. Information on education, major awards, design philosophies and quotes by either the artists themselves or their contemporaries hopefully enhance the sense of what Austrian design is and who the designers are. The accompanying illustrations reflect the most recent projects or objects by the architects and designers.

Alpenländische Veredelungs-Industrie Ges.m.b.H. (AVI) was founded in the 1950s. Today it is one of the largest producing companies of welded wire mesh mass-produced for the needs of an industrial clientele. The mesh is used principally as fencing material. On a lesser basis it is employed for gates and display systems, hanging racks and screens.

In the early 1980s, although clearly still concentrating on industrial production, AVI began to look for a new creative outlet for its product. Max Droschl (see photograph), then a manager at AVI, was put in charge of this project. He invited two other design firms who limited themselves to focussing on using the wire mesh, which would be coated in colors, for the creation of furniture. They began designing in 1983. Because the mesh construction did not permit water to collect, and because it was a lightweight, durable product, outdoor furniture became one of the main priorities for this material. The first designer was Alexander Korab, a young Viennese (born 1962) who had studied at the Hochschule für angewandte Kunst with Hans Hollein and later with Italian designers Ettore Sottsass and Alessandro Mendini. Korab designed the "Chaise Longue Lechos" (1983), the "Klisia Chair" (1983) and a bed (1985), illustrated in this book. The second design firm is called IDEEN, and they designed a number of garden pavilion variations. Droschl himself designed, amongst other things, the illustrated wardrobe (1984). In 1983, Korab received the Design Excellence award from the Austrian Product Show.

Although some of AVI's furniture designs are still in production or available on commission, the company is phasing out this activity. The main reason is that it is too costly for the European furniture market. AVI represents an excellent example of letting material inspire design and design products.

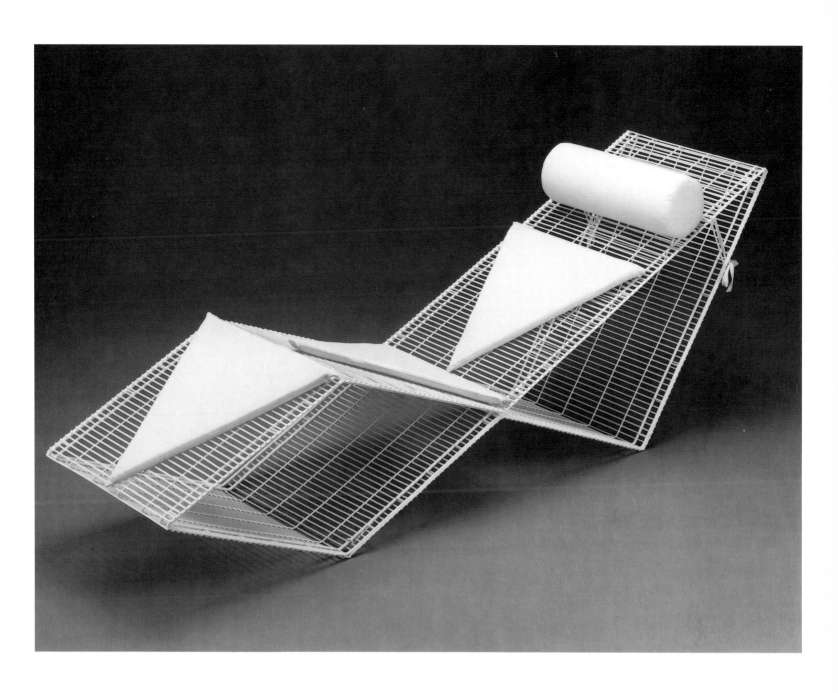

1. Max Droschl. (Photo: Helmut Utri)
2. Alexander Korab, Chaise longue "Lechos",
1983. Manufactured by AVI, Graz. Welded
wire mesh, fire lacquered in hepox-powders.
(Gift of AVI to The Art Institute of Chicago,
1986.206)

3. Alexander Korab, Chair "Klisia", 1983.
Manufactured by AVI. Welded wire mesh,
fire lacquered in hepox-powders.
4. Max Droschl, Wardrobe, 1984. Manufactured by AVI. Welded wire mesh, iron tube and
metal-sheets, fire lacquered in hepox-powders.
5. Alexander Korab, Bed, 1985. Manufactured
by AVI. Welded wire mesh, iron tube, fire lacquered in hepox-powders.

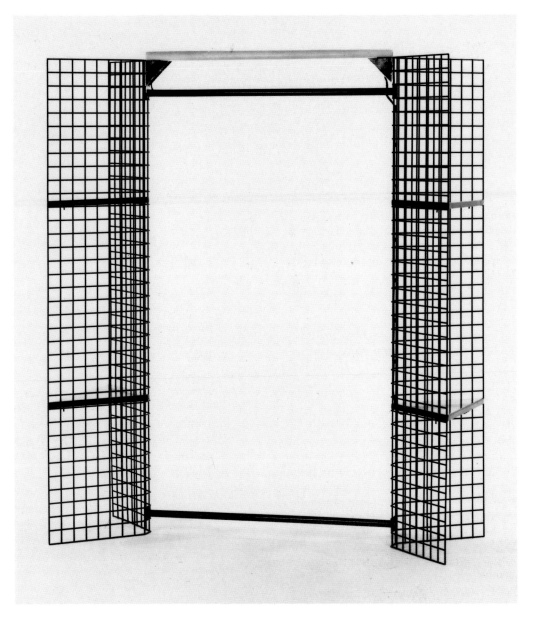

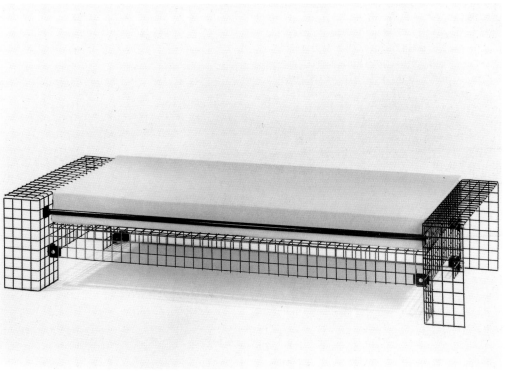

B.R.A.N.D.

B.R.A.N.D. is the company name for furniture and interior designers Boris Broschardt and Rudolf Weber. Born in 1958 in Rijeka, Yugoslavia, Broschardt attended nautical school before becoming a self-taught metal worker and designer. Weber, also self taught, was born in Vienna in 1955 and had previously attended technical school. As autodidacts Broschardt and Weber are representatives of a number of designers who have come to the discipline through a desire to create, unencumbered by the restrictions of a formal arts education. Both had previously worked in a metal factory.

In 1983, B.R.A.N.D. was formed, with their first exhibition two years later at Section N in Vienna. Since then, they have participated in numerous exhibitions, including *Wohnen von Sinnen* (1983), at the Kunstmuseum Düsseldorf, *Zwischen zwei Stühlen* (1983), in Bregenz, Austria, and an individual exhibition at the Ronni Kufferle Galerie, in Vienna in 1989. They have also completed a number of interior design projects, such as Black Market: a shop in Vienna which sells records, clothing and has a restaurant. The Vitra Museum in Weil-am-Rhein has two pieces in their permanent collection.

Since their formation they have developed three furniture systems; "Raumdezvous", "Arcus" and "Cosmo". Developed in 1985, "Raumdezvous" is a group of objects which acts not only as furniture, which they consider the "dumb servant of conventional use", but as a total environment. It is functional sculpture. Their subsequent design systems are based on a similar logic. The "Cosmo" system is created from the form of the circle. Modeled in five different sizes and cast into tubular steel, sections of the circle are combined with leather and wood to create the various components of the furnishing system. B.R.A.N.D. sign and certify each object, reinforcing the status of each work as more than a piece of furniture.

1. Boris Broschardt (left) and Rudolf Weber (right).
2. Boris Broschardt, Bookcase "Saturn" from the Cosmo Series, 1988. Manufactured by B.R.A.N.D., Vienna. Coated tubular steel and laminated plywood.

3. Modular environment system "Raumdezvous", 1985. Iron rods.
4. Chair from the "Raumdezvous" system,
1985. Iron rods and upholstery.

5, 6. Bookcases, 1985-86. Iron rods and glass.

Coop Himmelblau

Coop Himmelblau was formed in 1968 in Vienna by Wolf D. Prix, Helmut Swiczinsky and Rainer Michael Holzer who left the group in 1971. Prix, born in Vienna in 1942, and Swiczinsky, born in Poznan, Poland, in 1944, were both students of architecture at the Technical University in Vienna. Although principally involved in the creation of architecture, Coop Himmelblau has also turned its talents to design and fine arts. In 1987-88 they opened a second atelier in Los Angeles where they also teach at SCI-ARC (Southern California Institute of Architecture). Over the years Coop Himmelblau has lectured and been visiting professor around Europe, the United States, Japan and Australia.

Coop Himmelblau has, since 1968, presented a number of actions and exhibitions in Europe, the United Kingdom and the United States. Notable amongst these was their 1969 single exhibit at the Museum für angewandte Kunst, Vienna, a group exhibit of *Architectural Projects* in 1975 at the Museum of Modern Art in New York, and the 1976 group exhibit/action *Super Summer* in Vienna. In 1988 they were the sole Austrians selected for the Museum of Modern Art's show on Deconstructivism. They have quite recently won three large competitions; a town planning project for Melun-Senart outside of Paris, a renovation of the famous Ronacher Theater in Vienna and a major addition to the Gartenhotel Altmannsdorf outside of Vienna. Their endeavors in product design date only from the last two years. For Vitra design, they have developed the "Vodöl" armchair and for EWE a moveable kitchen.

The early philosophy of Coop Himmelblau was to build "architecture like clouds". A fantastic architecture with a soft edge, striving to make the inhabited world a bit more humane. Titles like "Living Cloud" (1968-72) and "Villa Rosa" (1968) characterized this period. After ten years of seeing a world become increasingly less receptive towards humanity, Prix and Swiczinsky wanted an "architecture that bleeds, that exhausts, that whirls and even breaks". Their new aggressive tone corresponded with a newly aggressive architecture, one which remains somewhat on the fringe to this day. Titles once again reflected the new approach: "Hot Flat" (1978-79) is typical of this period.

Their latest work reflects this recent quote: "Our architecture can be found where thoughts move faster than hands to grasp it."

1. Wolf D. Prix (left) and Helmut Swiczinsky
(right). (Photo: Gerald Zugmann)
2. Melrose I, Los Angeles, California, 1990.
Model. (Photo: Tom Bonner)

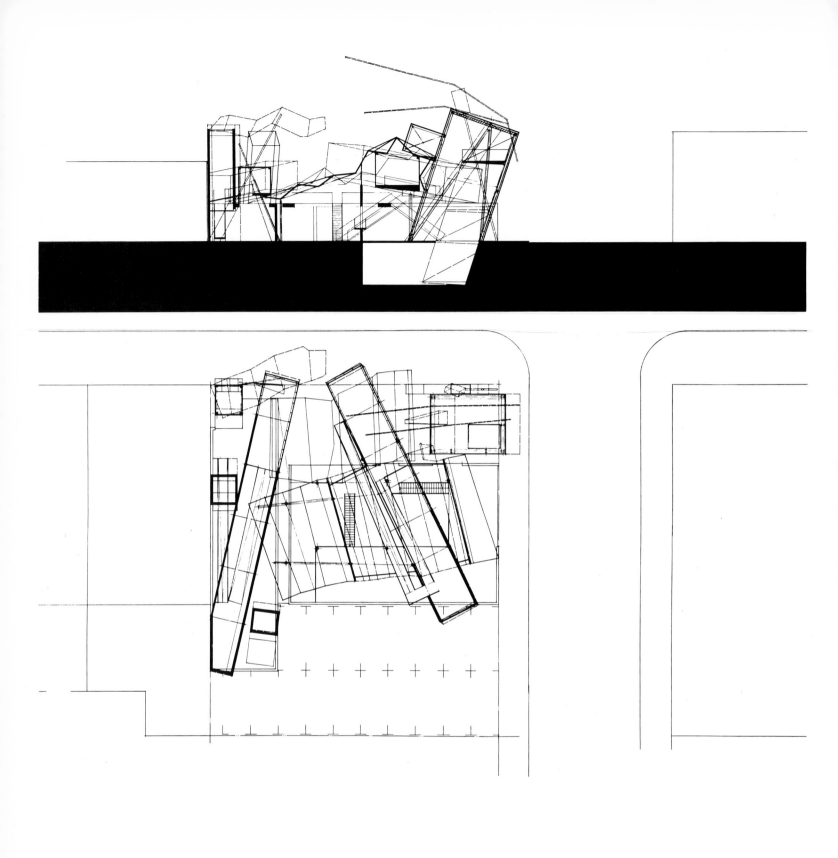

3, 4. Melrose I, Los Angeles. Section and plan.
5. Armchair "Vödol", 1989. Manufactured by
Vitra Edition. Painted steel, chromed tubular
steel and vinyl upholstery. (Photo: Studio/Frei)

ANSICHT SÜD

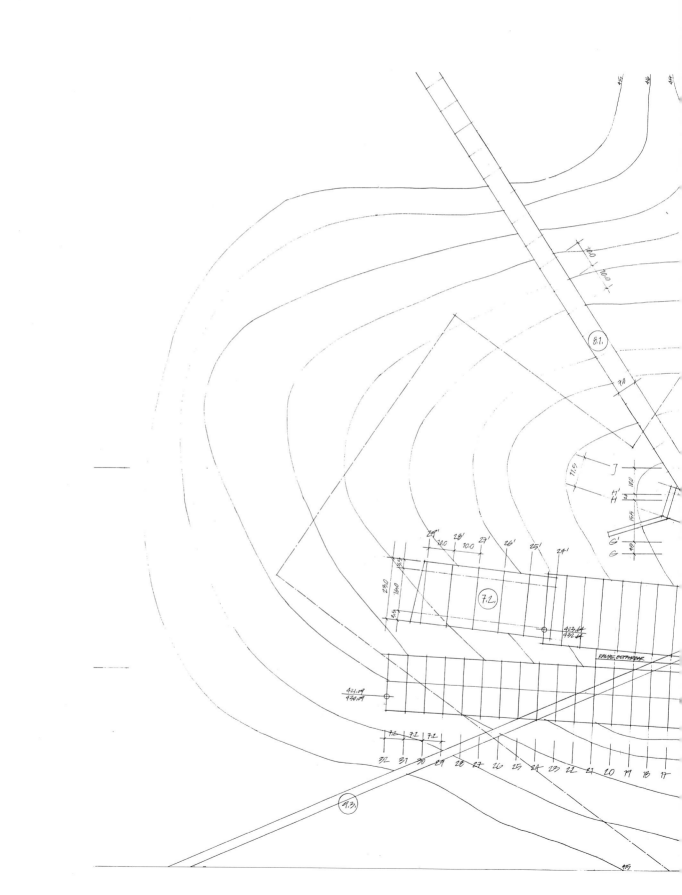

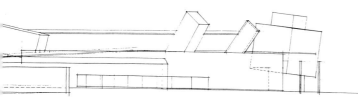

6, 7. Home and studio for Anselm Kiefer, Buchen, Germany, 1990. Elevation and site plan.

2,5   12,5   25 M

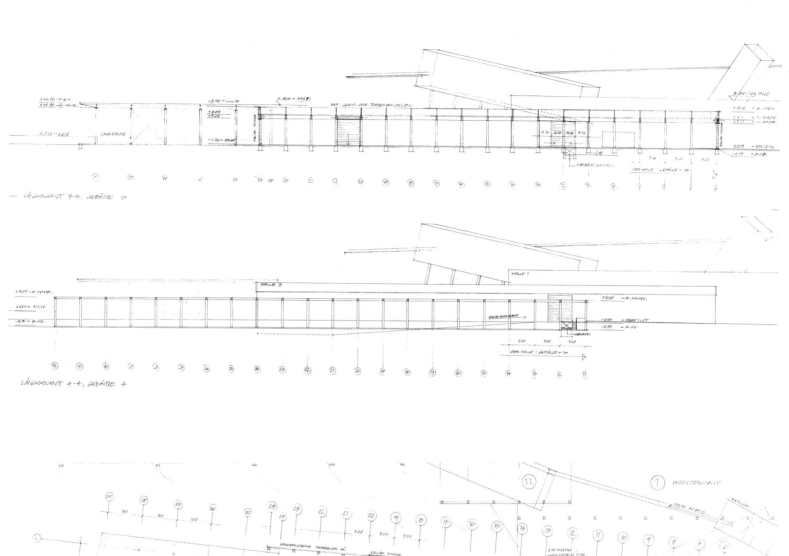

— LÄNGSSCHNITT 3-3, GEBÄUDE 3

LÄNGSSCHNITT 4-4, GEBÄUDE 4

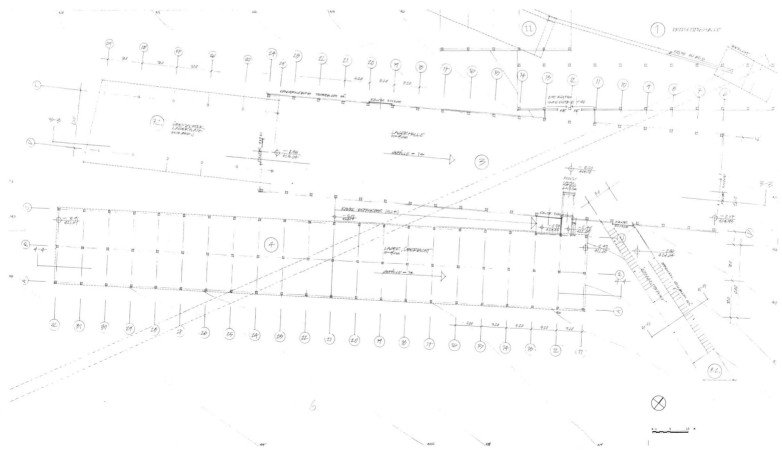

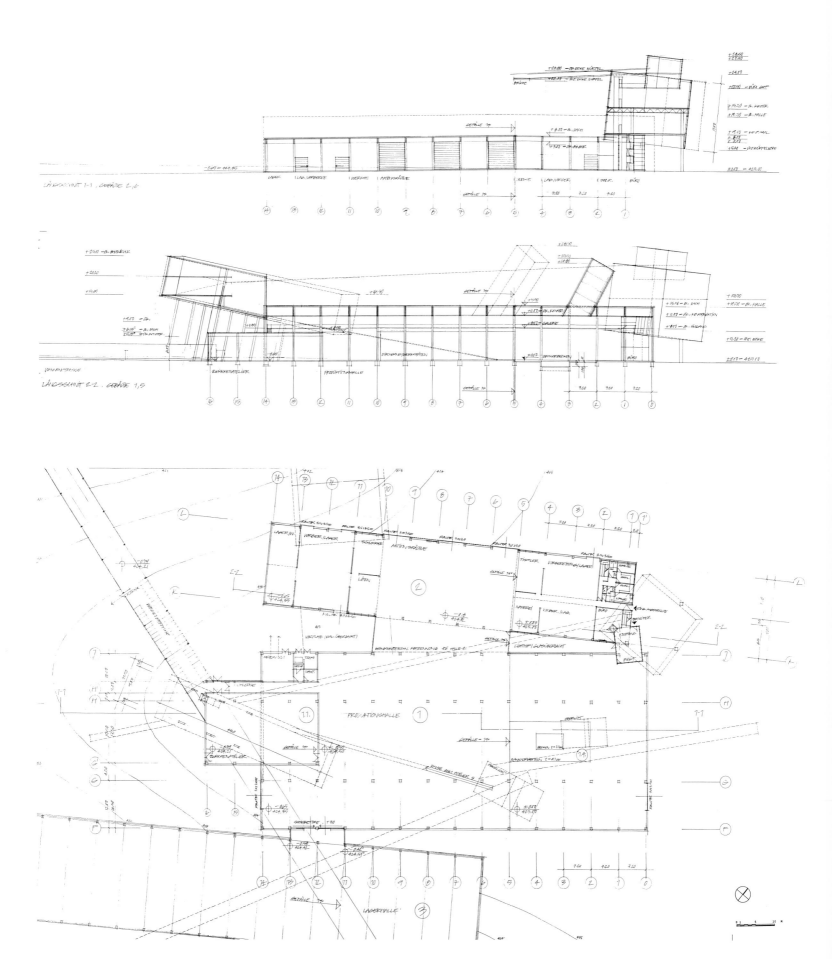

Günther Domenig

Born in 1934 in Klagenfurt, Austria, architect Günther Domenig studied at the Technical University in Graz. As both former student, former professor and former partner to a number of other Graz architects, he is considered one of the leaders of what is deemed the "Graz School". For ten years, from 1963 to 1973, he was in a partnership with Eilfried Huth, and later partnered Hermann Eisenköck. Since 1980, he has been professor at his alma mater.

As professor and lecturer he has been invited to numerous architectural centers, including Germany, Italy, France, the United Kingdom and the United States. Domenig has been part of many group and solo exhibitions; including *Urban Fiction,* Vienna (1969), *Medium Total,* Galerie nächst St. Stephan, Vienna (1970), *Transformations in Modern Architecture,* Museum of Modern Art, New York (1979), *Vision der Moderne,* Deutsches Architekturmuseum, Frankfurt (1986), *Günther Domenig,* Architectural Association London (1986), Oslo (1986), Brussels (1987), and *Günther Domenig: Das Stein-Haus,* Museum für angewandte Kunst, Vienna (1989). His most important prizes have been the Grand Prix International d'Urbanisme et d'Architecture, Cannes (1969) for his project Ragnitz, and he also received the Prix Européen de la Construction Métallique (1975).

Domenig's architecture has a decidedly sculptural flavor. In the 70s he made this statement in his undulating Z-Bank in Vienna, considered by many to be his masterpiece. Former students Michael Szyszkowitz and Karla Kowalski, now architects on their own, say that Domenig taught them "that for a building to be beautiful is enough". This is an understandably anti-intellectual response to an architectural community laden with self-styled intellects. One of Domenig's most recent works was a house for himself, called the "Steinhaus" or Stone-House. While it is possible to trace the development from the Z-Bank to the Steinhaus, it also reflects a nostalgic preoccupation with the mountains of Carinthia, around which he grew up.

1. Günther Domenig.
2. Addition to Funder factory 1, St. Veit an der Glan, Austria, 1987. Axonometric view.
3. Addition to Funder factory 1, St. Veit an der Glan. Model.
4. Addition to Funder factory 1, St. Veit an der Glan. Entrance. (Photo: Joachim Brohm)

pp. 88, 89
5. Addition to Funder factory 1, St. Veit an der Glan. Entrance ramp. (Photo: Joachim Brohm)
6. Addition to Funder factory 1, St. Veit an der Glan. View behind the undulating facade.

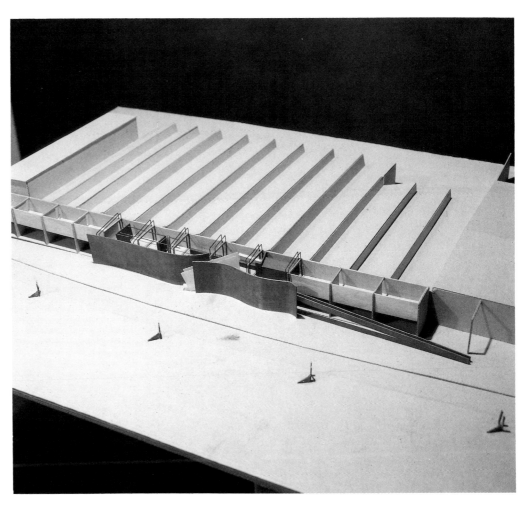

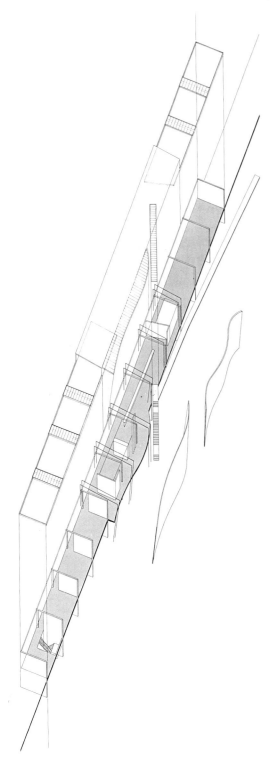

7. Addition to Funder factory 1, St. Veit an der Glan. Hallway. (Photo: John Zukowsky)
8. Addition to Funder factory 1, St. Veit an der Glan. Bar and moving display case in the lobby. (Photo: Joachim Brohm)
9. Addition to Funder factory 1, St. Veit an der Glan. View to the videobox. (Photo: Joachim Brohm)

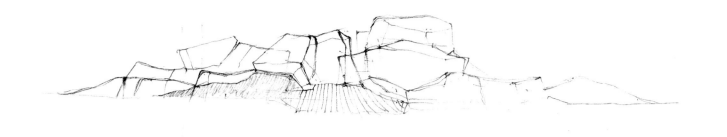

10. Steinhaus, Steindorf, begun 1986. Sketch.
11. Steinhaus, Steindorf. Aerial view.
12. Steinhaus, Steindorf. Site plan.

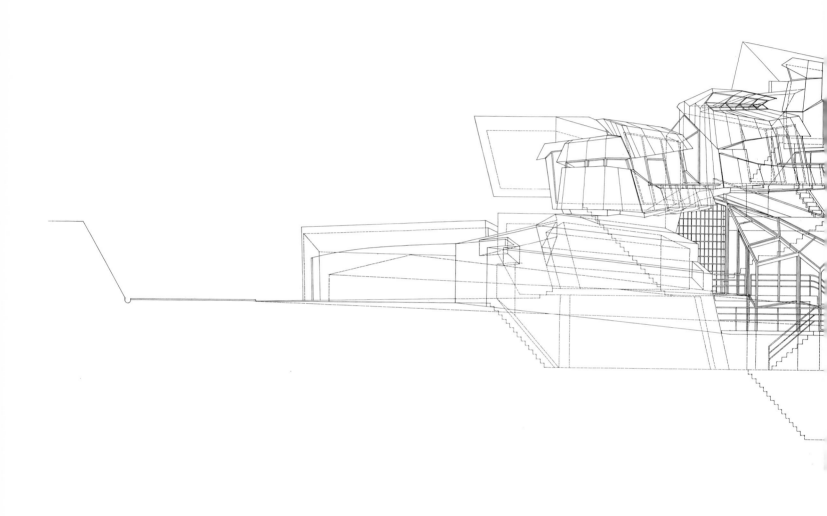

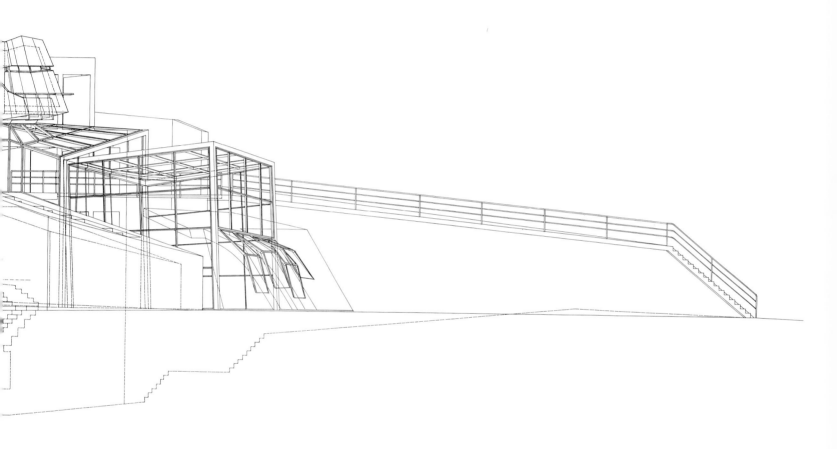

14. Steinhaus, Steindorf. View from the lake. (Photo: John Zukowsky)
15. Steinhaus, Steindorf. Wooden bridge. (Photo: John Zukowsky)
16. Steinhaus, Steindorf. Detail. (Photo: John Zukowsky)

Hans Hollein

Represented in his capacities as architect and designer, Viennese-born Hans Hollein has also been active in fine arts, teaching and publishing. Born in 1934, Hollein began his art studies in the Department of Civil Engineering at the Bundesgewerbeschule in Vienna. He then attended the School of Architecture at the Akademie der bildenden Künste in Vienna, receiving a diploma in 1956. From 1958 to 1959 Hollein studied architecture and planning with Mies van der Rohe at Chicago's Illinois Institute of Technology. He stayed in America to attend the College of Environmental Design at the University of California, Berkeley (1959-60), receiving his degree in 1960 as Master of Architecture. Since 1964, he has operated his own design atelier in Vienna.

Hollein's numerous awards began in 1966 with the Reynolds Memorial Award which he received for his renovation of the Retti candle shop in Vienna. He also received the Bard Award for excellence in Architecture and Urban Design in 1970, the Prize of the city of Vienna for Architecture, in 1974, the Grand Austrian State Award for Fine Arts in 1983, the Pritzker Architecture Award in 1985 and the Chicago Architecture Award in 1990, to name a few.

Hollein's design philosophy is encapsulated in his 1968 statement that "Everything is architecture". He has sought, in his architecture and designs, to break down conventional standards and paradigms in exchange for a new and all encompassing ideal of what architecture can be. His architecture would include aircraft carriers (Aircraft-carrier city in landscape, 1963), clenched fists (project for a skyscraper for Chicago, 1958), and crumbled paper (Fit in building, 1970). Hollein, the designer, is the Austrian most often associated with post-modern design and specifically the Italian design group Memphis. But, it is his own country's design history from which Hollein quotes with regularity. Adolf Loos and Otto Wagner are just two of the fin-de-siècle architects/designers whose modernist works and ideas have been "postmodernized". His most recent design, now in the development stage, is the Salzburg Museum, for which he won a 1989 international competition.

1. Hans Hollein. (Photo: Erich Pedevilla)
2. Haas-Haus, Stock-im-Eisen-Platz 4, Vienna,
1985-90.

3. Haas-Haus, Vienna. Site plan.
4, 5. Haas-Haus, Vienna. Plans (first floor and top floor).

pp. 102, 103
6. Haas-Haus, Vienna. Stairway.
7. Haas-Haus, Vienna. View into the atrium.
8. Haas-Haus, Vienna. Section.

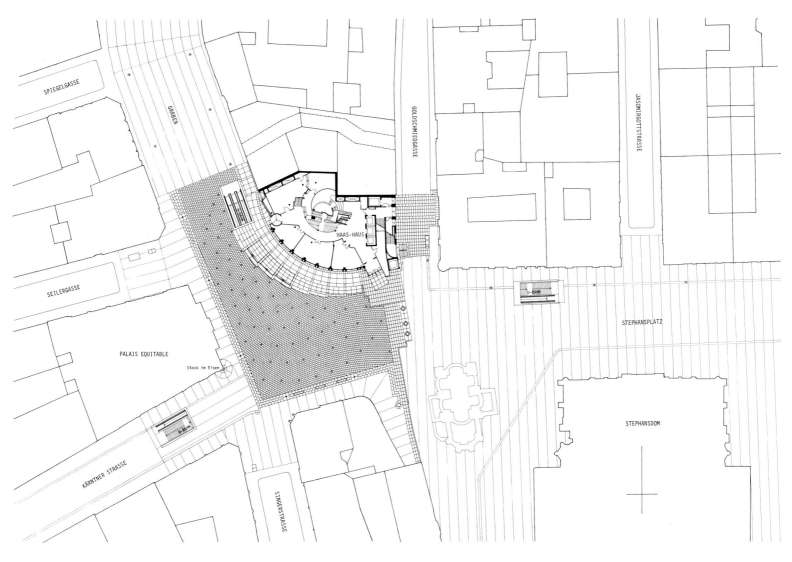

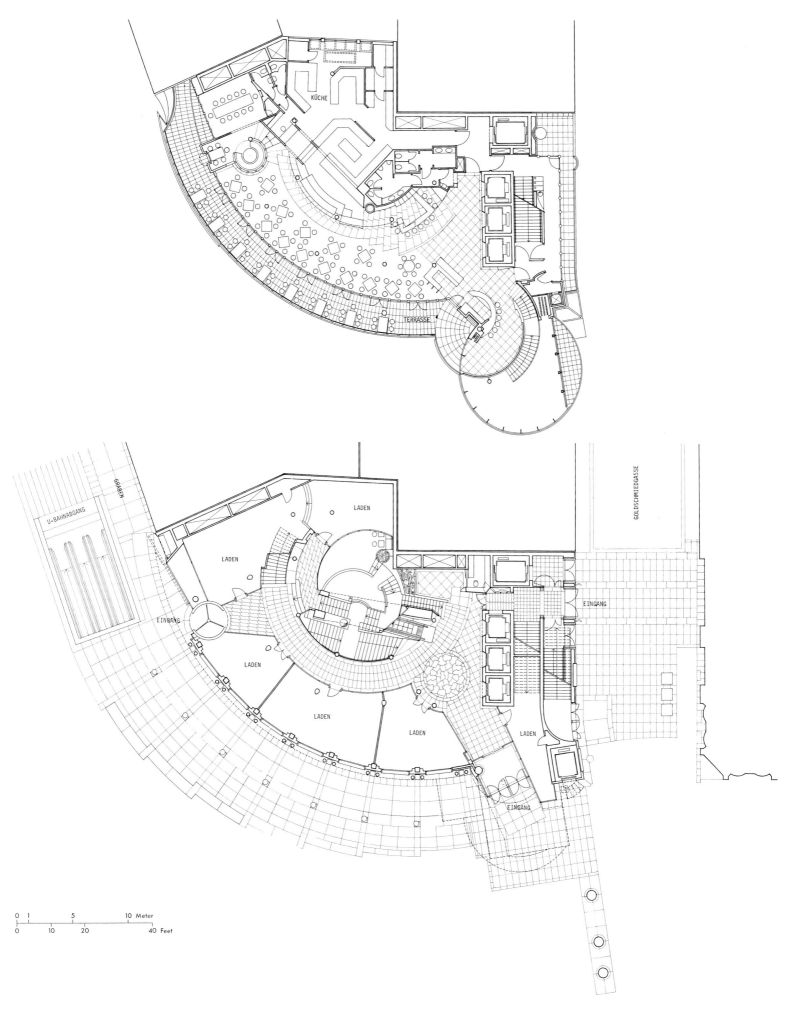

KÜCHE

TERRASSE

U-BAHNABGANG

GRABEN

GOLDSCHMIEDGASSE

LADEN

LADEN

LADEN

LADEN

LADEN

LADEN

LADEN

EINGANG

EINGANG

EINGANG

0 1   5   10 Meter
0   10   20   40 Feet

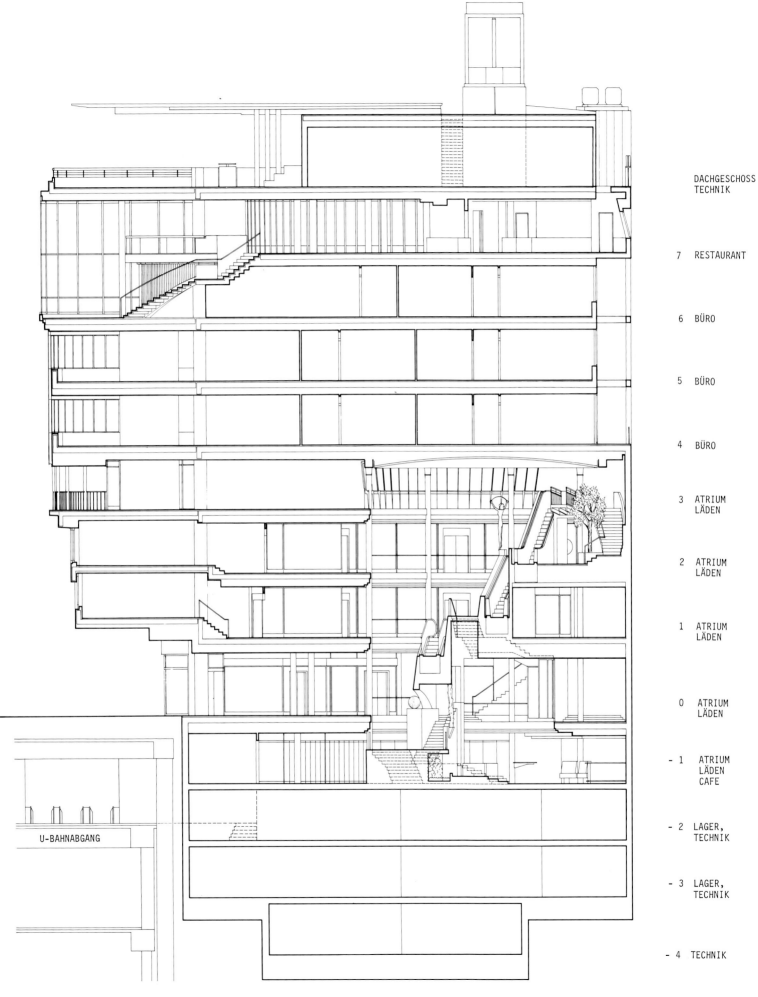

DACHGESCHOSS
TECHNIK

7 RESTAURANT

6 BÜRO

5 BÜRO

4 BÜRO

3 ATRIUM
LÄDEN

2 ATRIUM
LÄDEN

1 ATRIUM
LÄDEN

0 ATRIUM
LÄDEN

- 1 ATRIUM
LÄDEN
CAFE

- 2 LAGER,
TECHNIK

- 3 LAGER,
TECHNIK

- 4 TECHNIK

U-BAHNABGANG

9. Guggenheim Museum, Salzburg, project,
1989. Axonometric site plan.
10. Guggenheim Museum, Salzburg. Model.
(Photo: Georg Riha)

pp. 106, 107
11, 12. Guggenheim Museum, Salzburg. Plans.

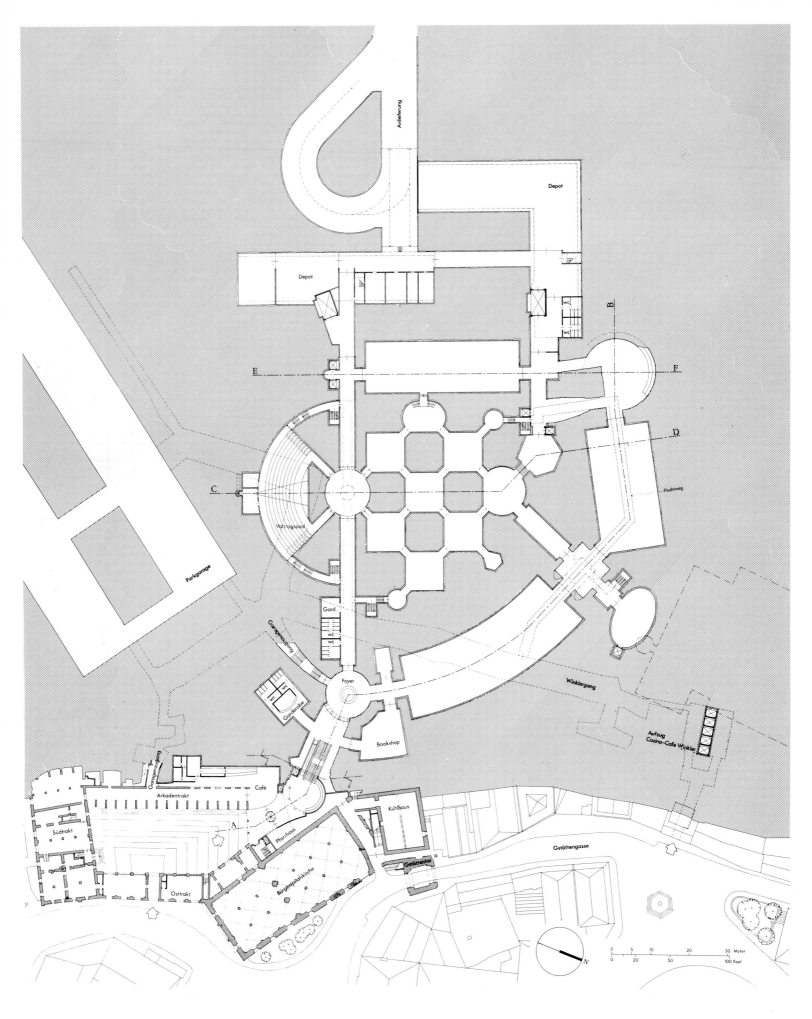

Anlieferung

Depot

Depot

WC

WC

B

E ————————————— F

D

C ————

Fluchtweg

Vortragssaal

Parkgarage

Gard.

WC

Garderobengang

Foyer

WC
WC

Garderobe

Winklergang

Aufzug
Casino-Café Winkler

Bookshop

Garagenzufahrt

Café

Kühlhaus

Arkadentrakt

A

Pfarrhaus

Südtrakt

Gnöttentor

Osttrakt

Bürgerspitalskirche

Gstättengasse

N

0   5   10   20   30 Meter
0   20   50   100 Feet

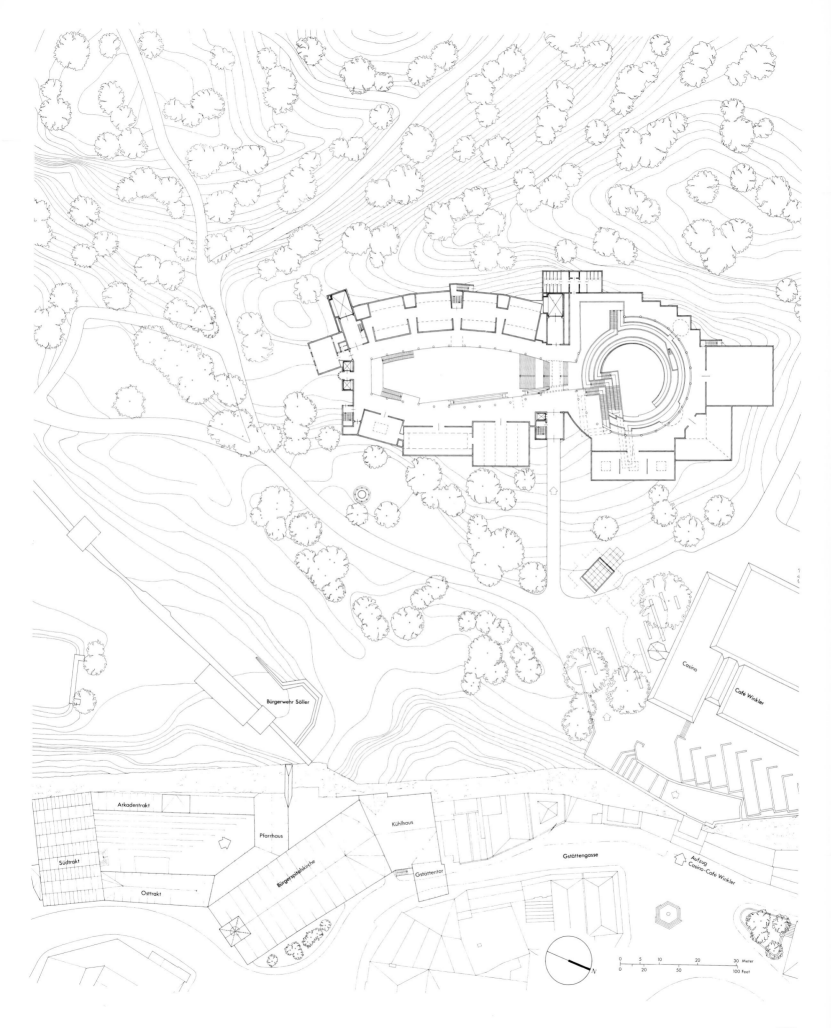

Bürgerwehr Söller

Arkadentrakt

Pfarrhaus

Kühlhaus

Südtrakt

Bürgerspitalskirche

Osttrakt

Gstattentor

Gstättengasse

Casino

Cafe Winkler

Aufzug
Casino-Cafe Winkler

0   5   10   20   30 Meter
0   20   50   100 Feet

N

107

13, 14. Guggenheim Museum, Salzburg.
Sections.
15. Guggenheim Museum, Salzburg. Model.
(Photo: Georg Riha)

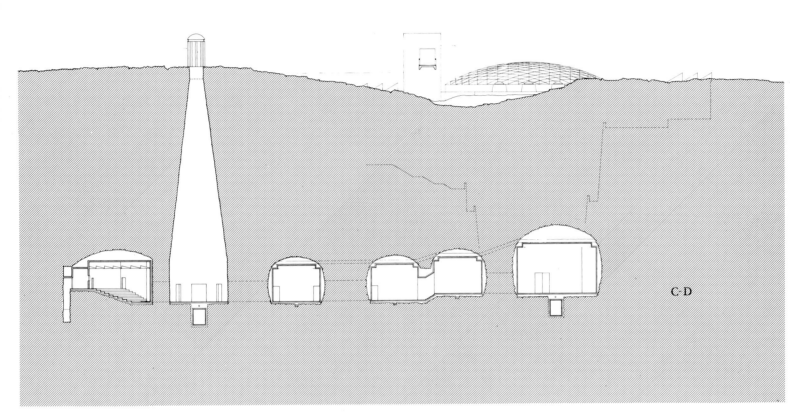

C·D

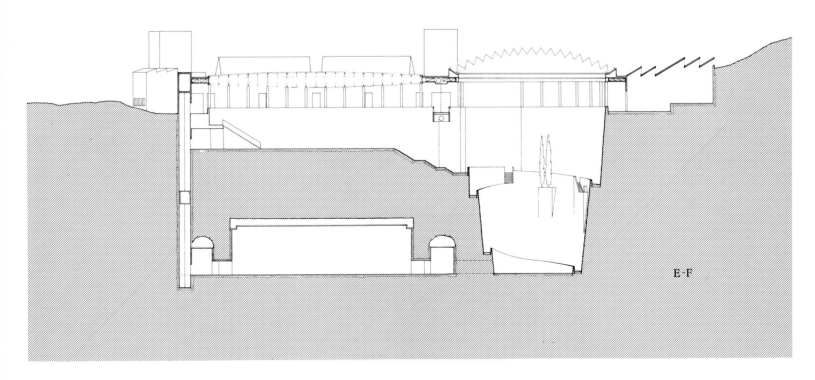

E·F

16. Grand Piano, 1990. Manufactured by
Bösendorfer, Vienna. (Photo: Dr. Parisini)
17. Grand Piano. Detail. (Photo: Dr. Parisini)

Fritz Maierhofer

Fritz Maierhofer was born in Vienna in 1941. He began his jewelry career in 1951, working as a traditional apprentice to Viennese jeweler Anton Heldwein. In 1965 he was given charge of the shop, and in 1966 he passed the Meisterprüfung in goldsmithing and silversmithing. The next two years were spent in London; first working for Andrew Grima, for whom he designed a watch collection manufactured by Omega, and later working as a freelance designer. It was here that he first began to experiment in acrylic, which he combined with gold and silver. 1970 marked a return to Vienna, along with his first exhibition in Salzburg. For the next sixteen years, Maierhofer stayed in Vienna, working and experimenting with different kinds of metal to create both jewelry and objects. In 1987 he went back to London after receiving a fellowship from the Sir John Cass College of Art. He returned to Austria in 1988, where he lives and works today.

Maierhofer, whose prolific exhibition record began in 1967, has been honored with a number of prestigious awards; these include prizes at the Viennese Art Foundation (1972), International Jewelry Competition in the Schmuckmuseum Pforzheim (1972), *Jablonec 87* (1987) and the Carinthian Private Galleries. In 1990 Maierhofer was awarded the Austrian Design Award Acknowledgment.

His work is in many public and private collections, including the Museum für angewandte Kunst, Vienna, the Schmuckmuseum Pforzheim, the Victoria and Albert Museum, London, and the National Museum of Scotland.

He has stated, "For me jewelry is a free form and visual expression. Our time teaches our Jewelry." As a medium to transmit messages, Maierhofer's jewelry can be seen as art. It is, for him, unimportant if his work is worn; scale cannot be seen as differentiating jewelry from sculpture. If time impacts upon the visual character of a work, then Maierhofer's experiences in London and Austria have been reflected in his work. The objects of the early sixties display the characteristic brash colors of London at this time. Likewise, ten years later the idyllic Austrian countryside embellished his work with a softer, more contemplative feeling.

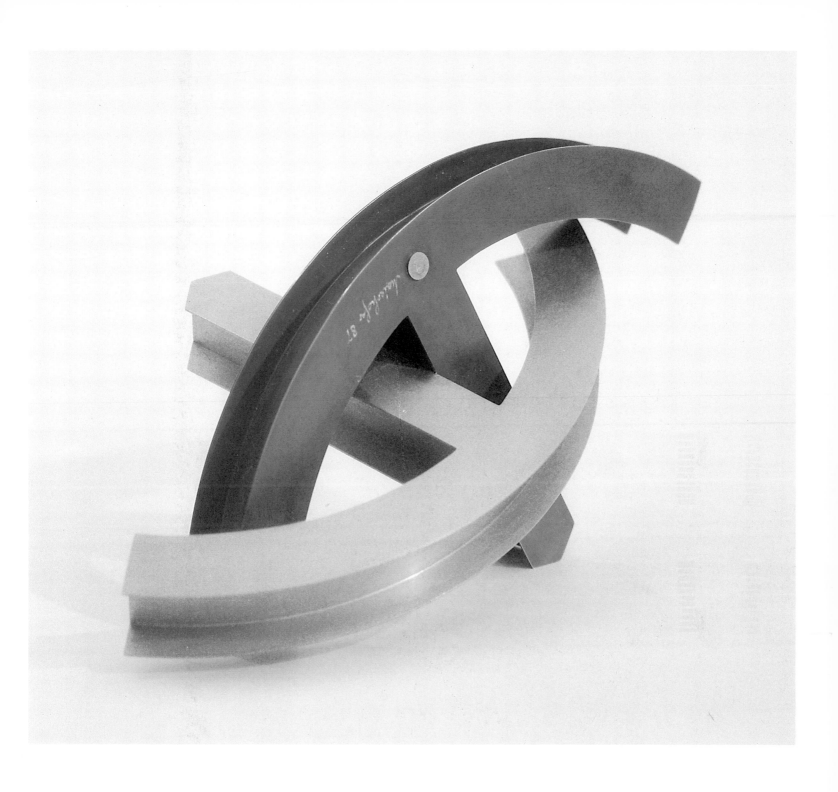

1. Fritz Maierhofer. (Photo: John Zukowsky)
2. Brooch, 1987. Yellow and oxidized gold.

3. Brooch, 1989-90. Silver oxidized and gold.
4. Brooch, 1989-90. Silver oxidized and gold.

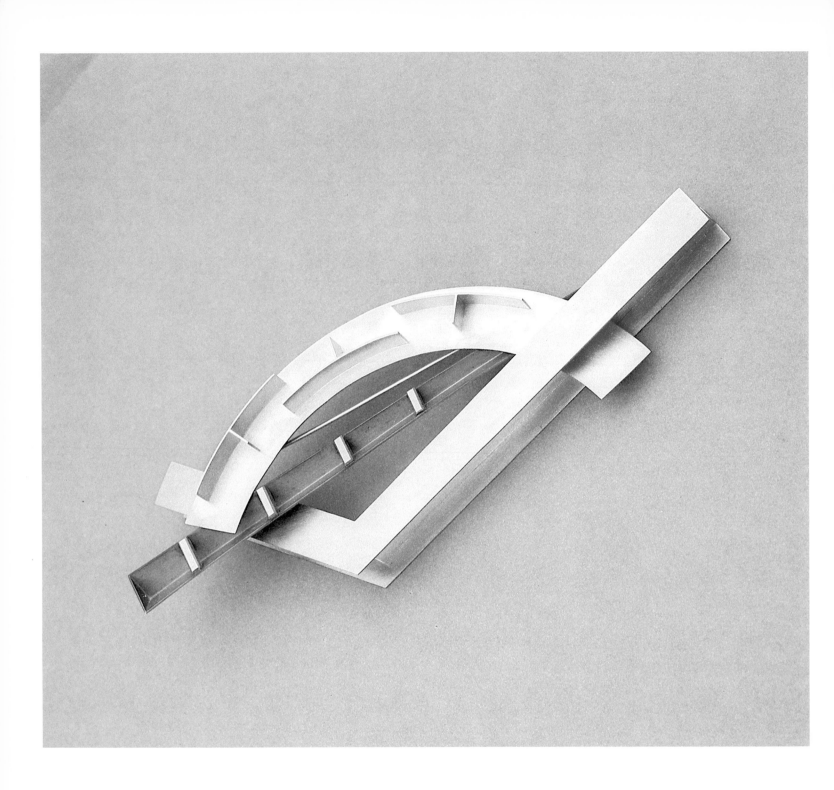

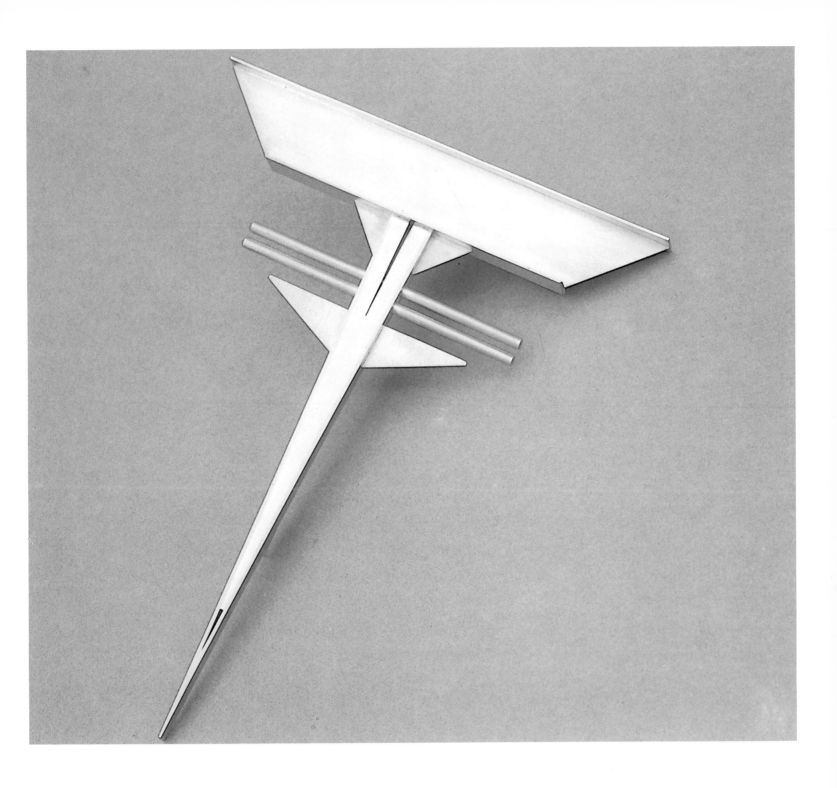

5. Brooch, 1987-88. Silver oxidized and gold.
6. Brooch, 1989-90. White and yellow gold.

Gert Mosettig

Jewelry artist Gert Mosettig was born in 1947 in Graz, Austria. In 1951 his family moved to Sweden where he remained until 1963 when he returned to Graz. In 1970 Mosettig left his native city for Vienna, and the Hochschule für angewandte Kunst. For the next five years he studied ceramics under Leinfellner, but received no degree in Fine Arts. As an artist and creator of jewelry, Mosettig refers to himself as an autodidact. He has lived and worked in Vienna since 1970. Mosettig's work can be seen in public collections of the Museum für angewandte Kunst in Vienna, the Deutsches Goldschmiedehaus in Hanau, Germany, and the National Gallery of Victoria in Melbourne, Australia.

Mosettig's approach to jewelry making is as untraditional as Fritz Maierhofer's is traditional. Self taught, he need not feel the burden of a professor's influence or past tradition. He assumes what can be seen as a technological stance towards his creations. Impetus derives from within the studio, which is filled with tools and machinery not usually associated with his craft. Deriving aesthetic pleasure from the appearance of these tools as well as geometric form, it is quite natural that Mosettig utilizes many semi-manufactured articles in his work. He does not use any precious or semi-precious materials.

Paradoxically, his design philosophy is one which does not stress workmanship. Design, he says, should not be reduced to the incidental. Thus, it is natural for him to spend two weeks thinking about a piece and one day creating it. Like the designer Werner Schmidt, Mosettig creates designs that offer hidden access for the wearer. The jewelry must be understood before it can be worn, and it must be worn. Having designed his creations for the purpose of ornament and not as object art, Mosettig says of his jewelry that it can only function if a person is wearing it, and not vice versa. In other words, a person can function without jewelry, but Mosettig's jewelry cannot function without people.

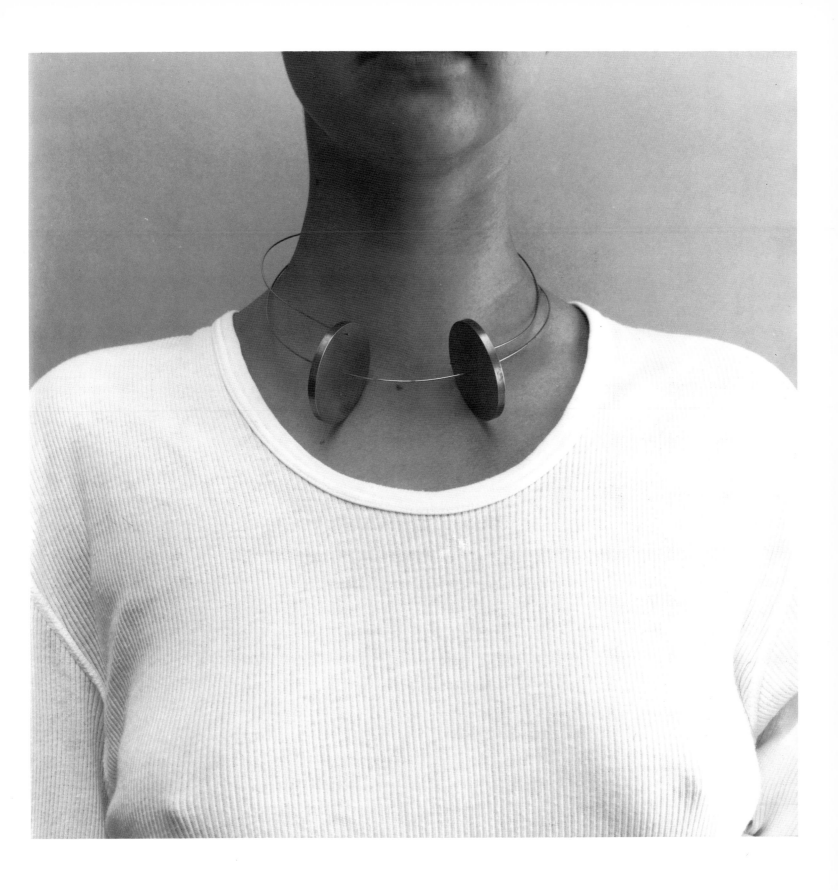

1. Gert Mosettig's studio. (Photo: Peter Dressler)
2. Necklace, 1986. Brass and steel.

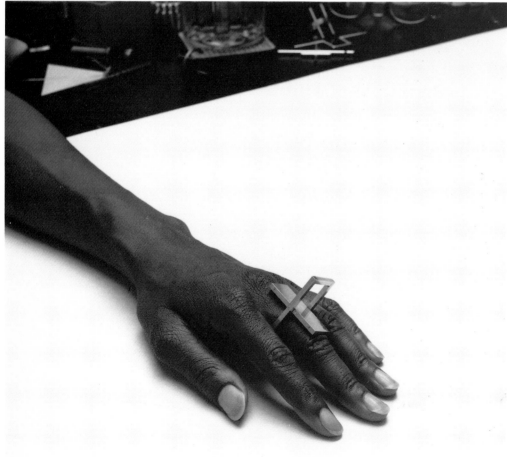

3, 4. Ring. Brass.
5, 6. Ring, 1978. Aluminium in two pie

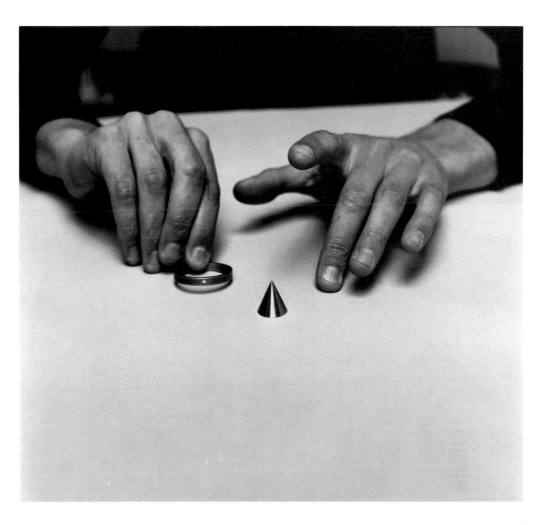

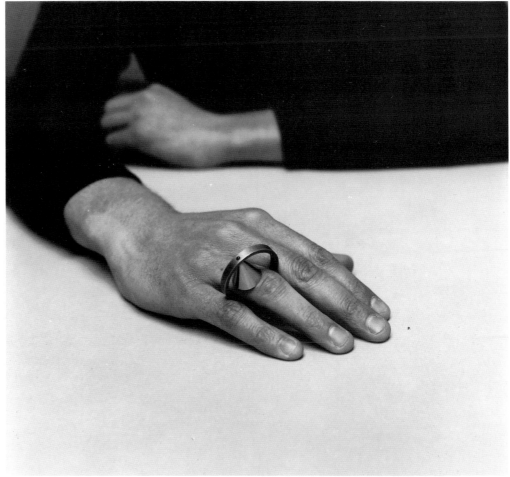

7. Table lamp, 1989-90. Brass.
8. Hanging lamp, 1989-90. Brass.

Gustav Peichl

Architect Gustav Peichl was born in Vienna in 1928. From 1949 to 1953 he studied in the Meisterklasse (graduate program) at the Akademie der bildenden Künste in Vienna under Clemens Holzmeister. His awards include the Prize of the city of Vienna for Architecture (1969), the Austrian State Award (1971), the Reynolds Memorial Award (1975), the Mies van der Rohe Award (1986) and the Architecture Prize for the city of Berlin (1989). He is also a member of the Austrian Arts Council, an honorary member of the Society of German Architects (since 1985) and an honorary member of the Royal Institute of British Architects, RIBA (since 1987). Peichl has had a number of books published about his work.

"To me the occupation with BUILDING is: pondering, putting ideas to work, drawing, constructing and realizing." With a no-nonsense statement such as this, Peichl seems to be the most straightforward of all the included architects. In the 1960s Peichl pioneered theories about flexibility and growth potential, but has essentially remained quite traditional in his building approach.

When thinking about a project, he simultaneously visualizes in his head and sketches his ideas. These sketches he continually refers to when creating a final draft.

Peichl is aware of architecture's influence on the humanity it confronts daily, even if they are not. That is why he feels it is the architect's job to tackle these problems. The architect must use his rational and emotional sides to confront these problems. He feels that architecture must find a comfortable place between art and purpose to be successful. His more recent designs include the extension to the Städel museum, Frankfurt (1987-90), his long-range project of Studios for Austrian Radio (ORF) in Dornbirn, Innsbruck, Linz and Salzburg (1968-72), Graz and Eisenstadt (1979-81), and the beautiful Kunstforum in Vienna (1989). Still under design development and soon to be constructed is the EVN communications center in Maria-Enzersdorf near Vienna.

1. Gustav Peichl. (Photo: Barbara Kramp)
2. Städel museum addition, Frankfurt, 1987-90. Model. (Photo: Schwingenschlögl)
3. Städel museum addition, Frankfurt. Sketch for the main entrance.

4. Städel museum addition, Frankfurt. East elevation. (Photo: Monika Nikolic)
5. Städel museum addition, Frankfurt. Main entrance. (Photo: Helmuth Heistinger)

pp. 128, 129
6. Städel museum addition, Frankfurt. Entrance hall. (Photo: Monika Nikolic)
7. Städel museum addition, Frankfurt. Exhibition space. (Photo: Monika Nikolic)

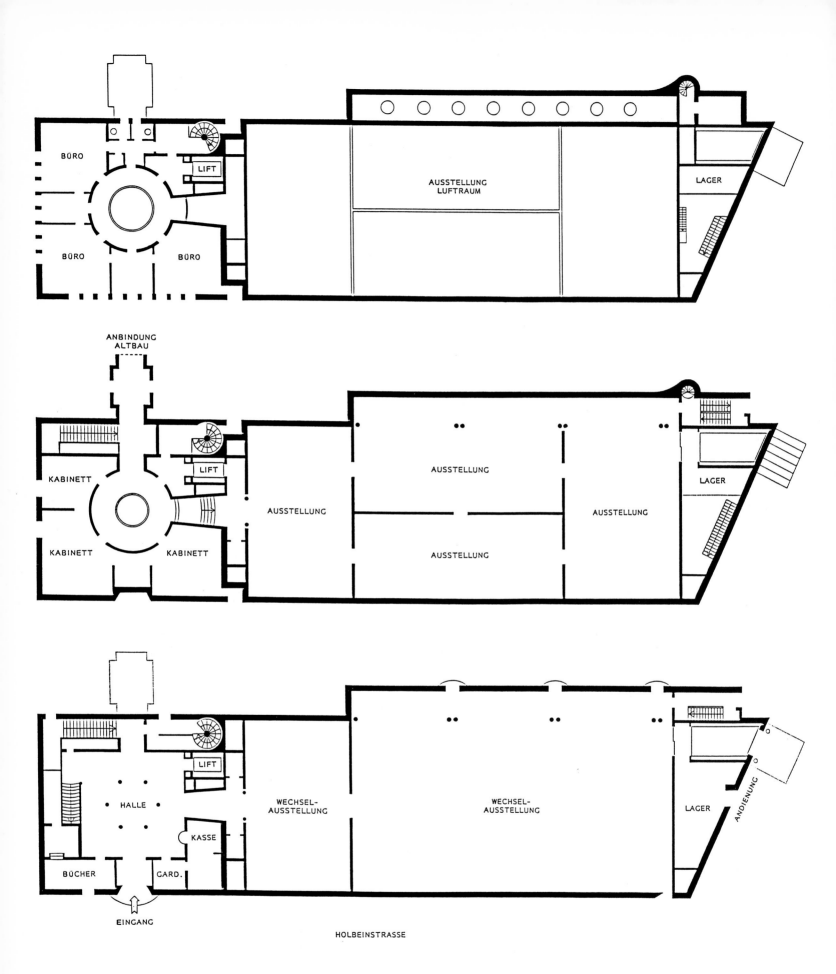

BÜRO

BÜRO

BÜRO

LIFT

AUSSTELLUNG
LUFTRAUM

LAGER

ANBINDUNG
ALTBAU

KABINETT

KABINETT

KABINETT

LIFT

AUSSTELLUNG

AUSSTELLUNG

AUSSTELLUNG

AUSSTELLUNG

AUSSTELLUNG

LAGER

LIFT

HALLE

KASSE

BÜCHER

GARD.

EINGANG

WECHSEL-
AUSSTELLUNG

WECHSEL-
AUSSTELLUNG

LAGER

ANDIENUNG

HOLBEINSTRASSE

130

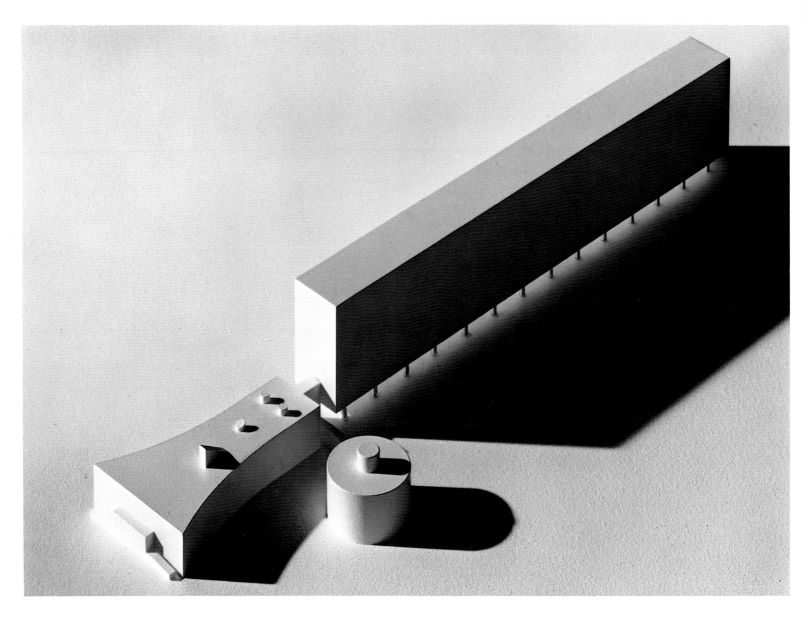

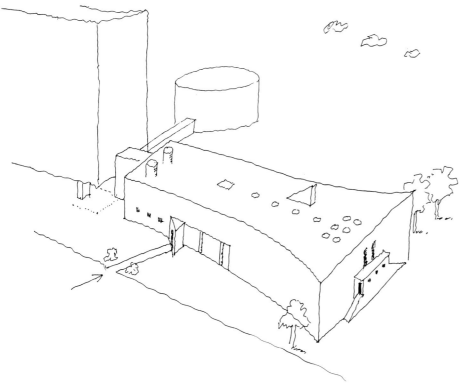

12. EVN communications center, Maria-Enzersdorf, near Vienna, 1990. Model. (Photo:
Schwingenschlögl)
13. EVN communications center, Maria-Enzersdorf. Sketch.
14. EVN communications center, Maria-Enzersdorf. Plan.

pp. 134, 135
15. EVN communications center, Maria-Enzersdorf. Model. (Photo: Schwingenschlögl)
16. EVN communications center, Maria-Enzersdorf. Perspective study of the interior.
17. Cartoon, 1991.

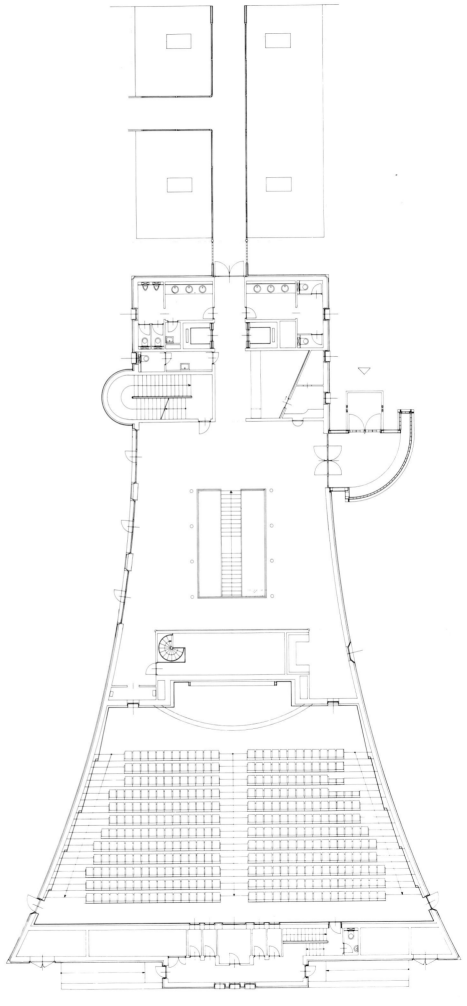

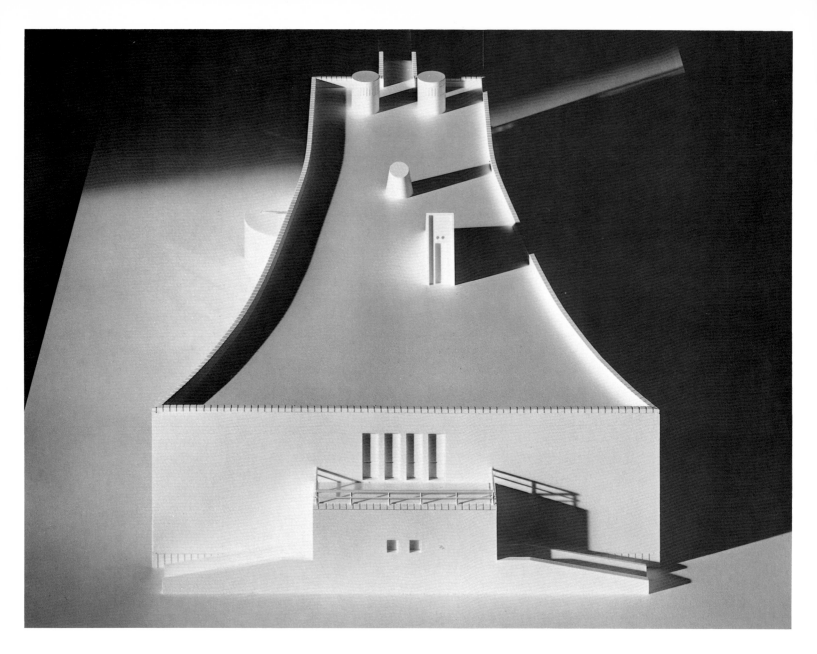

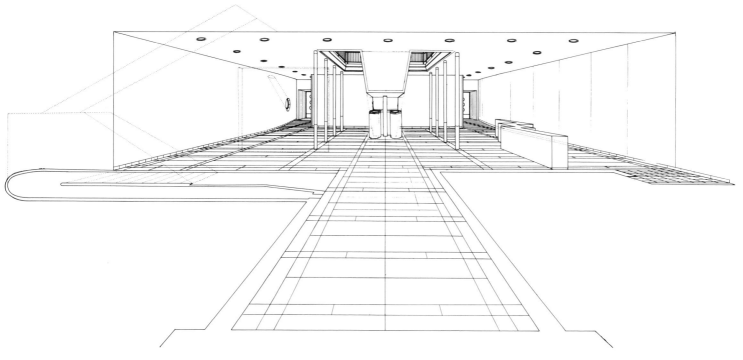

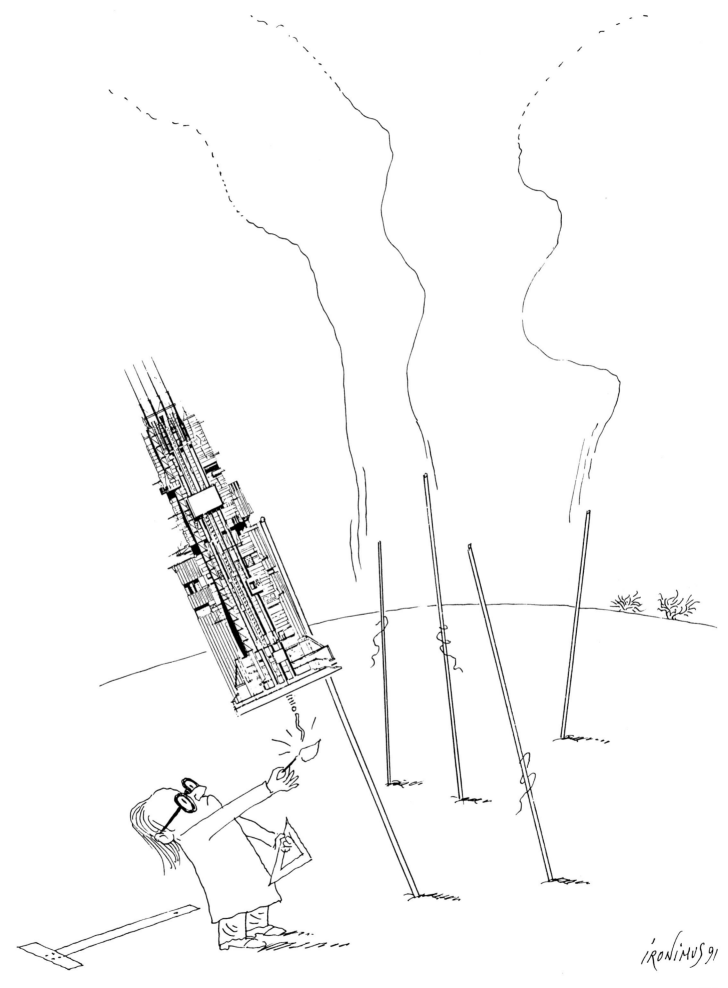

Ferdinand Alexander Porsche

The founder of Porsche Design G.m.b.H., F.A. Porsche comes from a family long associated with European design. He was born in 1935 in Stuttgart, Germany. During the war years his family moved to Zell-am-See in Austria. In 1954 he began his studies as an apprentice with Bosch, both in their workshop and in their technical design office. In 1957 he attended the famous Hochschule für Gestaltung in Ulm, after which he joined Porsche AG, the family business which produces the well-known automobiles. In 1962, he took over the leadership of their design studios, and in 1963 under his direction they developed the popular Porsche models "904" and "911".

It was in 1972 that he broke off to begin the separate company of Porsche Design, in Stuttgart. Then in 1975 the company moved to Zell-am-See. Today, the firm is one of the leading design companies in Europe with a team of nine designers working together; it represents a more international approach to design and economics, in that few of the products are actually manufactured in Austria. Manufacturers in Germany, Italy and Japan all produce designs by Porsche. The products, which range from cookware to lighting to motorcycles, can be found around the world.

Porsche feels that good design can be described by the phrase "liberties and limits", which was the title of the 1987 show of the firm's work at the Centre Pompidou in Paris. The liberties are the designer's imagination and instinct. The limits are the purpose, function and material relative to the work in question. While there are design philosophies which can be universally applied, each piece creates a new set of problems which must be individually tackled. For example, because Porsche is against designs which put appearance over function, black is the color – or absence of color – which he prefers. It is universal. It allows the design to be the essence in the user's or viewer's perception. But, design is not all aesthetics and function. It is also form and comfort, or how an object responds and feels. Purity and clarity of form, functionality and an innovative approach in problem solving are all trademarks of Porsche's designs.

1. Ferdinand Alexander Porsche.
2. Telephone, 1989. Manufactured for the
German Federal Postal Administration.

3. Television set "M55-911", 1989. Manufactured by Grundig AG.

4. Washing machine "Supernova", 1989. Manufactured by Eudora.

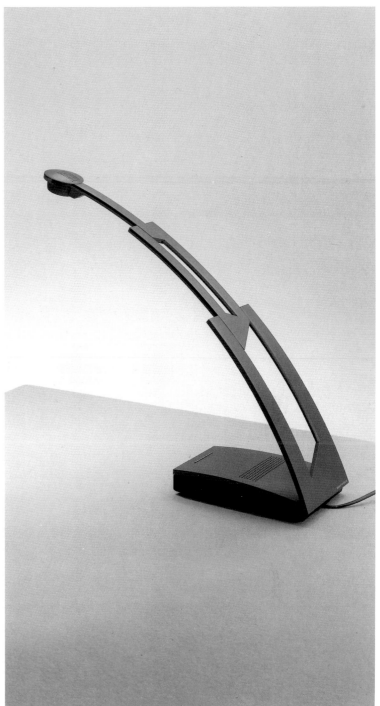

5. Steering wheel, 1984. Manufactured by
Mitsubishi.
6,7. Lamp "Jazz", 1989. Manufactured by PAF.
Halogen lamp. (Photo: Aldo Ballo)

Werner Schmidt

Born in 1953 in Trubbach, Switzerland, architect and designer Werner Schmidt completed a training course as a mason, before turning to the study of building architecture. In 1972 he began a study course at the Technical School for Engineering in Winterthur, Switzerland, earning a degree as an architect in 1978. This same year he supervised two major building projects. Between 1982 and 1987 he further studied architecture with Hans Hollein at the Hochschule für angewandte Kunst in Vienna. He received his diploma in 1989, graduating cum laude as a Magister Architecturae. The same year he opened his atelier for Architecture and Design in Disentis, Switzerland.

Schmidt, who has been in exhibits since 1985, has already received a number of impressive awards and prizes. In 1985 his collapsible chair, "Faltsessel", won first prize in a competition organized by the German furniture company Vitra Ltd. and the Hochschule für angewandte Kunst, Vienna, in 1987 his metal "Toy Lamp" won a second place in Vienna, while in 1989 he was awarded an appreciation prize by the Austrian Federal Ministry of Science and Research, for outstanding artistic achievement. He has also participated in a number of important exhibitions including the 1985 *Biennale of Architecture* in Venice, in which he showed plans for a new "Ponte dell'Accademia", the 1986 *Wohnlust* exhibition at the Künstlerhaus in Vienna and the 1987 Christmas show, *Schau wie schön* in Vienna. His work has also been shown in a number of galleries in Germany and Austria.

Like Porsche Design, innovation is one of Schmidt's main goals. But, where there is instantaneous recognition of Porsche's objects, Schmidt's are a little less easily discernible. He says he is looking for "new, different realities that might be existing, hidden in everyday objects and waiting to be perceived," and this is what he forces the user and viewer of his work to do. Once the object has been identified, the functional qualities of the work become clear; easy setup, limited spatial needs for storage and the ability to move and manipulate with facility. What Schmidt sees himself creating are essentially new objects with seemingly impossible solutions.

1. Werner Schmidt.
2-5. "Klapptisch" (folding table), 1986. Aluminium.

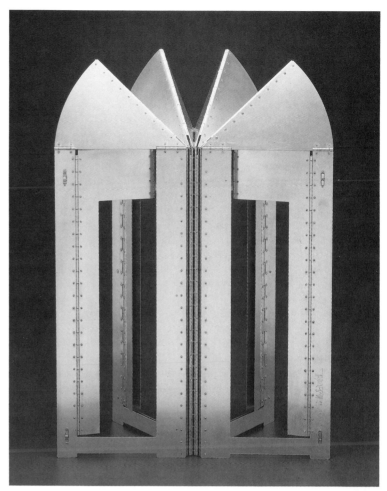

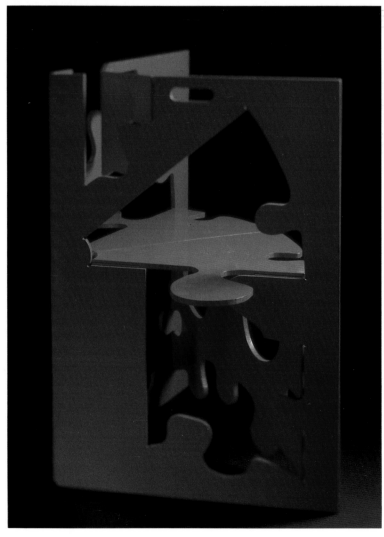

144

6, 7. "Jig-saw puzzle chair", 1985. Painted plywood.
8-11. "Rolladenstuhl", 1988. Wood and metal.

Heinz Tesar

Architect Heinz Tesar was born in Innsbruck, Austria in 1939. Between 1961 and 1965 he studied at the Akademie der bildenden Künste, Vienna, in the Meisterklasse for architecture with Roland Rainer. He received his diploma in 1965. Tesar worked in Hamburg (1959-61), Munich (1965-68) and Amsterdam (1971), before becoming a member (1972-77) of the governing body of the Austrian Society for Architecture. Since 1973 he has been an independent architect with his atelier in Vienna. Tesar has been awarded the Prize of the Zentralvereinigung der Architekten Österreichs four times (1965, 1979, 1986, 1988), the Austrian Prize for Fine Arts in 1982 and the Prize of the city of Vienna for Architecture in 1983. He has been invited around the world as a visiting professor and honored with no less than eight personal exhibitions.

Feeling that architecture is a dialogue between stimulation and reflection, it is not surprising that Tesar's projects harken back to the turn of the century architects who made Vienna a design center. One of his more recent buildings, Schömer-Haus, is both modernist, in function and structure, and nostalgic, in its elaborate inside covered by an unassuming facade. Asked to give a definition of architecture, Tesar would say "Architecture is at the same time a compliment of time, place, cause and mode"; this is what he has implemented for his prominent patrons.

In creating a project, Tesar utilizes water color drawings to think through his ideas. It is his way of recording and discovering both design and the design process. Besides the Schömer-Haus, his other recent projects include a rooftop apartment for a violinist in Linz (1985-90), a stage for the papal visit, Salzburg (1988), a kindergarten in Vienna (1990) and the successful competing entry for a municipal building in St. Gall, Switzerland (1990).

1. Heinz Tesar. (Photo: Hansueli Trachsel)
2. Sabaini rooftop apartment, Linz, Austria,
1985-90. The apartment's roof.

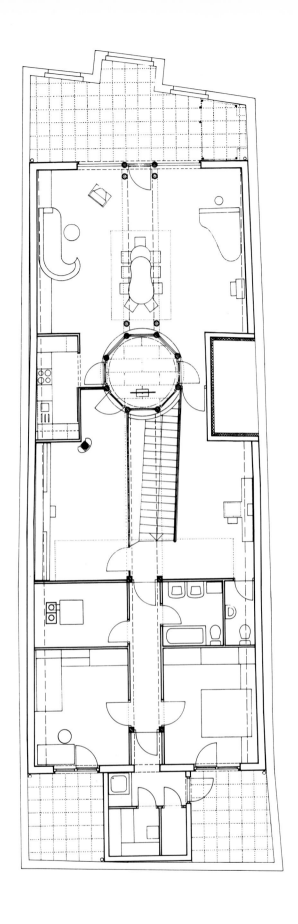
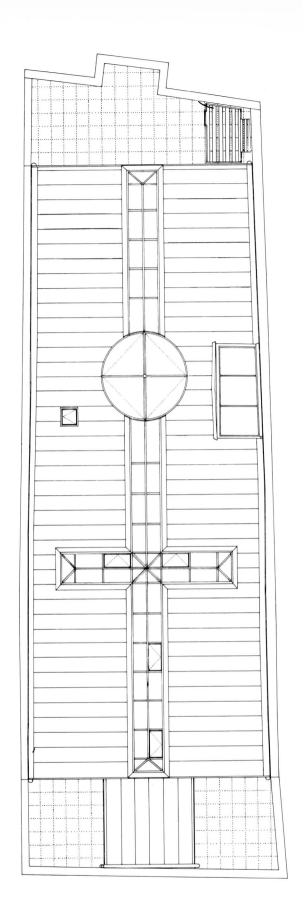

148

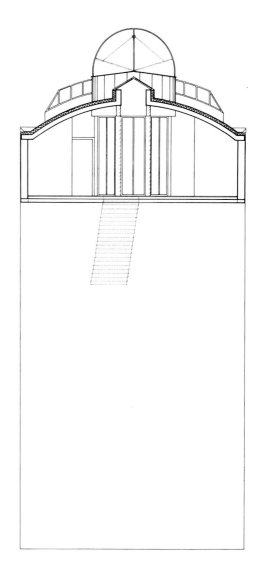

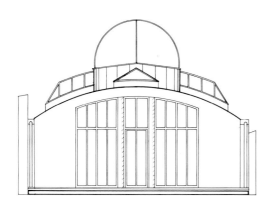

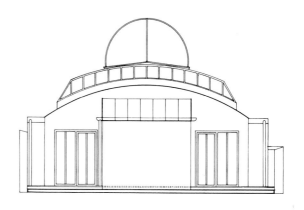

3, 4. Sabaini apartment, Linz. Plans.
5-8. Sabaini apartment, Linz. Elevations and
section.

149

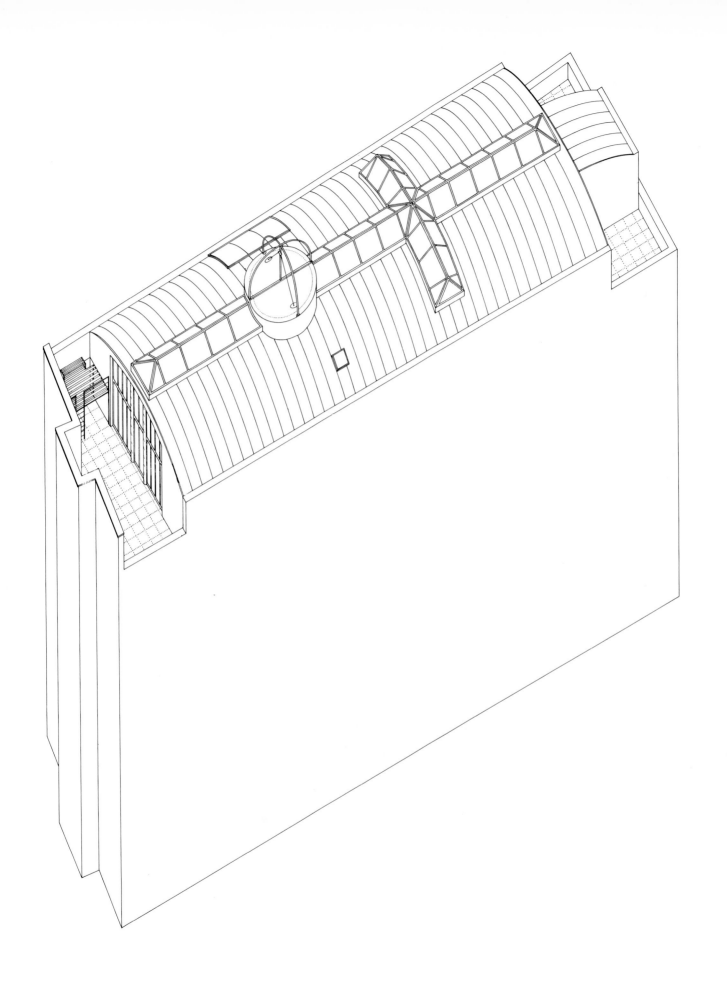

9. Sabaini apartment, Linz. Axonometric view.
10. Sabaini apartment, Linz. Interior looking toward the entrance.

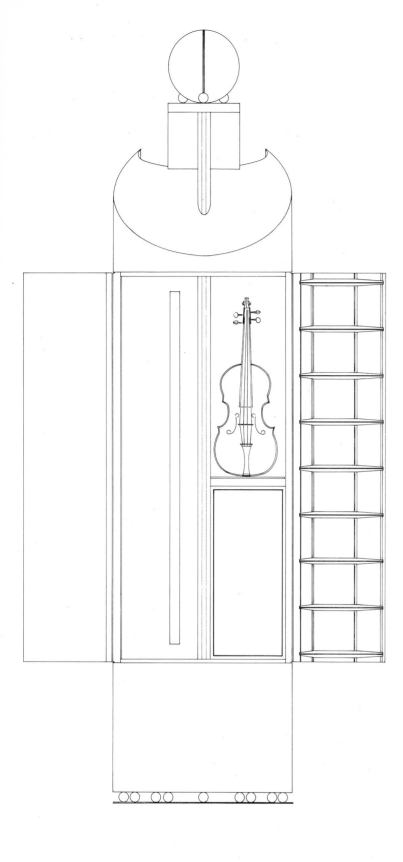

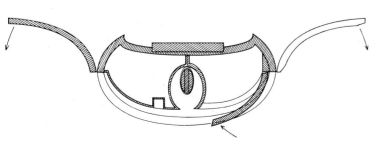

11, 12. "Stradivari" violin case, 1989. Elevation and plan.
13. "Stradivari" violin case with open doors.

14. Office building and police station, St. Gall,
Switzerland, 1989. Model. (Photo: Hann)

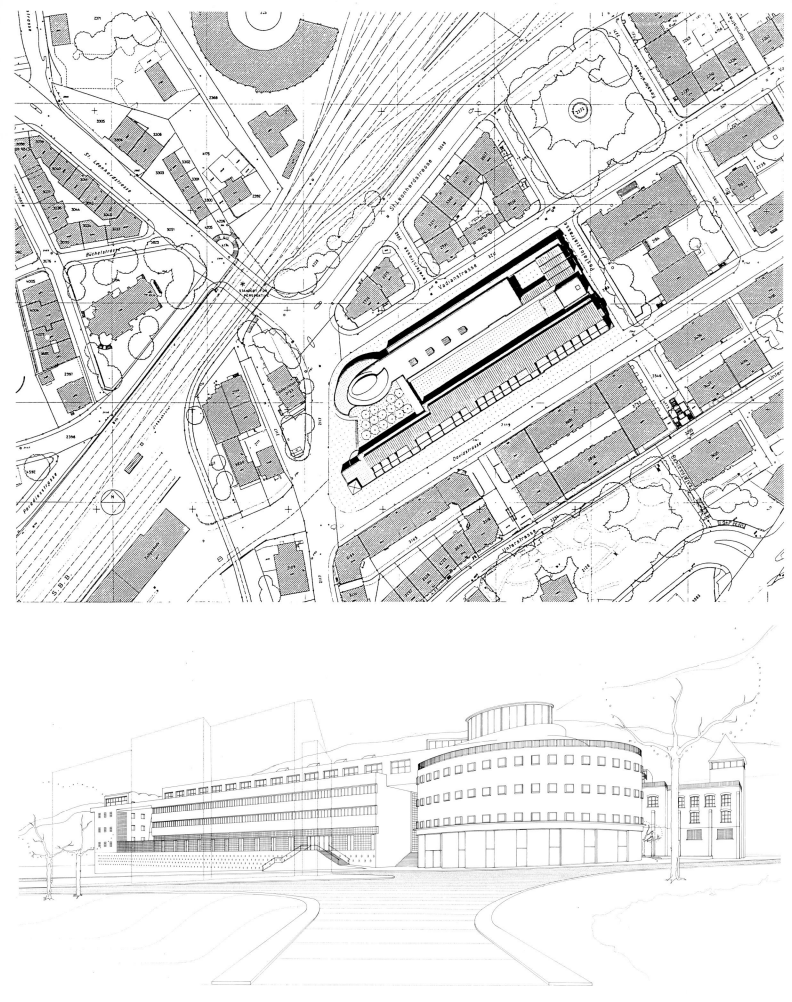

15. Office building and police station, St. Gall. Site plan.
16. Office building and police station, St. Gall. Perspective view.
17. Skyscraper "Chicago", based on the police station in St. Gall. Computer projection.
18, 19. Police station (head building), St. Gall. Axonometric view and plan.

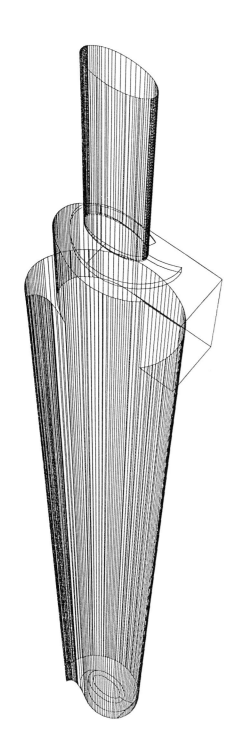

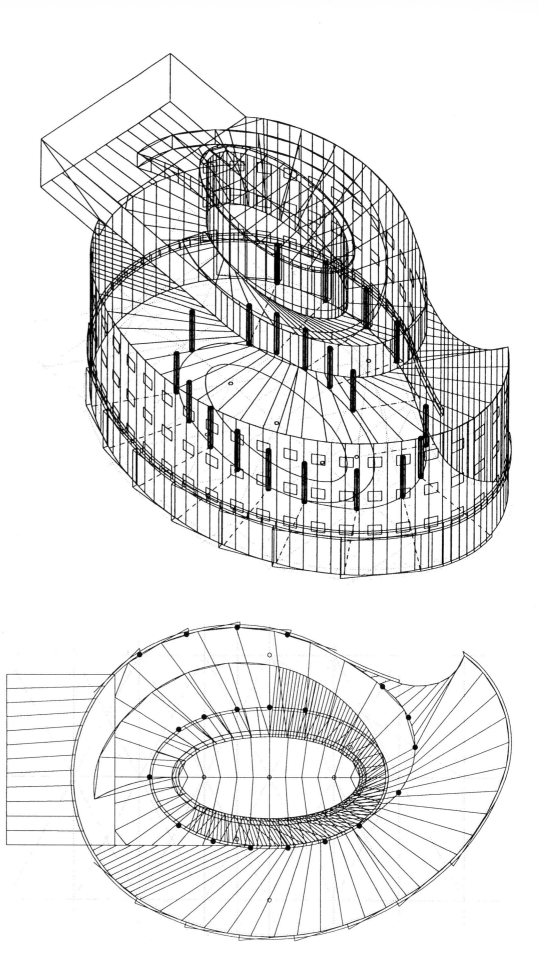

Michael Wagner

Architect and designer Michael Wagner was born in Bad Berleburg, Germany. He studied architecture at Aachen University from 1973 to 1975, and fine arts at the Ecole des Beaux-Arts in Paris from 1976 to 1977, receiving his diploma in 1979. From 1982 to 1988, Wagner was assistant professor at the Akademie der bildenden Künste in Vienna. He then resigned his position, in order to devote himself full-time to the design and creation of furniture and interior spaces. He currently lives and works in Vienna.

In 1989 Edition W G.m.b.H. was formed, essentially as a venue for new furniture design. At this time Wagner is the only designer, but there is the hope that it will serve as an outlet for contemporary international product design. Wagner has received much critical acclaim for his work, including a 1989 mention at the Austrian State Prize for good design. His work has also been included in many important design exhibitions and competitions, among them the IBA (Internationale Bauausstellung), Berlin in 1981. Wagner was also chosen to participate in *Design Wien* at the Museum für angewandte Kunst in Vienna, *Design aus Österreich* at the Wohnbühne in Munich and *Design dall'Austria* in Trieste, all representing overviews of contemporary Austrian design.

Wagner defines the design aesthetic for his Edition W metal furniture with the phrase "Less is more," first coined by Mies van der Rohe. It is achieved by a reduction of the whole to the most essential of parts. But functionalism, in terms of the user's convenience, is never sacrificed for the sake of the reduced aesthetic. Wagner wants to use his furniture to improve the quality of home life. To paraphrase his ideas, he hopes to reduce the physical and psychological burdens of the user, in order to allow new spatial conceptions and uses of living space. Material and mobility are the two main factors which allow this reconstitution of space to take place. Steel plate has the advantage of easy manipulation and visual dematerialization which allows the object to be perceived as background. Wheels, attached to most of Wagner's designs, reinforce the works' ability to change a space through functional dynamism.

1. Michael Wagner. (Photo: Jo Pesendorfer)
2. Movable container "graficar", 1989.
Manufactured by Edition W, Vienna. Folded
sheet-metal in epoxy powder, silver finish.
(Photo: Jo Pesendorfer)

3. Wardrobe "Morgan", 1988. Manufactured
by Edition W, Vienna. Silver stove enamelled
folded sheet-metal. (Photo: Jo Pesendorfer)
4. Telephone table "Phone", 1988. Manufactured by Edition W, Vienna. Folded sheet-metal
in epoxy powder, silver finish and glass top.
(Photo: Jo Pesendorfer)

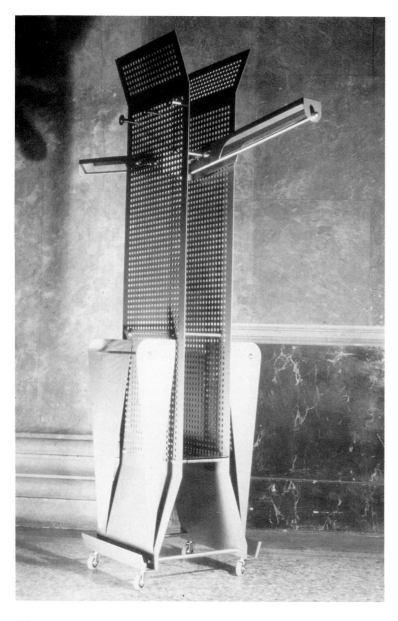

5. Stool "Sit down", 1985. Manufactured by
Edition W, Vienna. Folded sheet-metal in
epoxy powder finish. (Photo: Jo Pesendorfer)

Selected Bibliography

Achleitner, Friedrich: *Österreichische Architektur.* Salzburg: Residenz Verlag, 1980.

Anderton, Francis: "Haus of Tesar". *The Architectural Review,* Dec. 1988, pp. 30-33.

Architektur aus Graz. Bruxelles: C.I.A.U.D., 1987.

Architektur in Graz: 1980-1987. Graz: Verlag Droschl, 1987.

Blundell Jones, Peter: "Domenig Directions". *The Architectural Review,* Dec. 1988, pp. 73-79.

Collins, Michael: *Towards Post-Modernism: Design since 1851.* London: British Museum Publications, 1987.

Collins, Michael, and Andreas Papadakis: *Post-Modern Design.* New York: Rizzoli, 1989.

Coop Himmelblau: *Architecture is Now.* New York: Rizzoli, 1983.

Davey, Peter: "Complexes of Hollein". *The Architectural Review,* Dec. 1988, pp. 39-45.

Design und Objekte aus Österreich. Österreichisches Museum für angewandte Kunst, Vienna, 1987.

Design Wien. Österreichisches Museum für angewandte Kunst, Vienna, 1989.

Dormer, Peter: *The New Furniture: Trends and Traditions.* London: Thames and Hudson, 1987.

Emery, Marc: *Furniture by Architects.* New York: Harry N. Abrams, 1988.

Feuerstein, Günther: *Visionäre Architektur: Wien 1958/1988.* Berlin: Ernst & Sohn, 1988.

Fonatti, Franco: *Gustav Peichl: Opere e Progetti 1952-1987.* Milan: Electa, 1988.

Frampton, Kenneth (ed.): *A New Wave of Austrian Architecture.* The Institute for Urban Studies, New York, 1980.

Fritz Maierhofer: Gold und Silberschmied. Galerie Am Graben/Inge Asenbaum G.m.b.H., Vienna, 1982. Text by Fritz Maierhofer and Inge Asenbaum.

Grazer "Schule". Architektur-Investitionen. Graz: Akademische Druck- u. Verlagsanstalt, 1986. Text by Dietmar Steiner.

Guggenheim Museum Salzburg: Ein Projekt von Hans Hollein. Salzburg: Residenz Verlag, 1990. Text by Hans Hollein, Thomas Krens and Wieland Schmied.

Günther Domenig: Das Steinhaus. Österreichisches Museum für angewandte Kunst, Vienna, 1988. Text by Peter Noever.

Gustav Peichl. Royal Institute of British Architects, London, 1989.

Hans Hollein. Sezon Museum of Art, Tokyo, 1987. Text by Arata Isozaki.

MAN transFORMS. Vienna: Löcker Verlag, 1989. Text by Hans Hollein.

Kapfinger, Otto: "Utopia and Image". *The Architectural Review,* Dec. 1988, pp. 46-50.

Kapfinger, Otto, and Franz Kneissl: *Dichte Packung: Architektur aus Wien.* Salzburg: Residenz Verlag, 1989.

Koller, Gabriele. *Die Radikalisierung der Phantasie: Design aus Österreich.* Salzburg: Residenz Verlag, 1987.

Kräftner, Johann: *Bauen in Österreich.* Vienna: Edition Christian Brandstätter, 1983.

Margolin, Victor (ed.): *Design Discourse.* Chicago: University of Chicago Press, 1989.

Meisterschule Gustav Peichl: Akademie der bildenden Künste, Vienna. Galerie Aedes, Berlin, 1987. Text by Hans-Peter Schwarz and Gustav Peichl.

Mosettig. Deutsches Goldschmiedhaus, Hanau, 1989. Text by Hartwig Kräutler.

Nakamura, Toshio (ed.): *Hans Hollein.* Tokyo: A+U Publishing, 1985.

Pettena, Gianni: *Hans Hollein: Opere 1960-1988.* Milan: Idea Books, 1988.

Prix, Wolf D., and Helmut Swiczinsky: *Coop Himmelblau.* Darmstadt: Verlag Jürgen Häusser, 1990.

Ramshaw, Wendy: "Eine Welt im Umbruch". *Art Aurea,* March 1990, pp. 86-90.

Sarnitz, August: *Lois Welzenbacher.* Salzburg: Residenz Verlag, 1989.

Städel: Der Museumserweiterungsbau von Gustav Peichl. Salzburg: Residenz Verlag, 1990. Text by Hans-Joachim Ziemke.

Steiner, Dietmar: *Architektur in Wien.* Vienna: Georg Prachner, 1984.

Thackara, John (ed.): *Design After Modernism.* London: Thames and Hudson, 1988.

All illustrations not credited as to their source are courtesy of the architects and designers.